Sacred Secrets

Finding Your Way to Joy, Peace and Prosperity

Sacred Secrets

Finding Your Way to Joy, Peace and Prosperity

EDITED BY PAULA GODWIN COPPEL

First edition 2007

To place an order for a Unity product or publication, call the Customer Service Department at 1-800-669-0282 or 816-251-3580 or visit us online at *www.unityonline.org.*

Cover design by Mark Szymanski

Interior design by Karen Rizzo

Bible verses have been referenced wherever possible. Where not referenced, the verses have been left as submitted by the authors.

Bible Reference Key:
KJV—King James Version
NRSV—New Revised Standard Version
RSV—Revised Standard Version

ISBN 978-0-87159-322-1
LCCN 2007936979

*To the people of Unity
who love and live these principles,
and to spiritual seekers everywhere
discovering the Truth within.*

Contents

Contents

Contents

Acknowledgements

It took a village to birth this book—Unity Village. The publisher wishes to thank the authors listed in the Table of Contents, whose biographical sketches appear on the Contributors pages, for the generous contribution of their inspiring essays and their steadfast support for the creation of *Sacred Secrets*.

We gratefully acknowledge the Unity House editorial board and production team for their hard work and commitment to this project: Charlotte Shelton, Phillip Pierson, Ellen Debenport, Adrianne Ford, Lisa Pruyn, Daniel Rebant, Sharon Sartin, Karen Rizzo, Joann Simcoe, Lila Herrmann, Peter Harakas, Elaine Meyer and MaryEllen Davis. We also wish to thank Michael Bernard Beckwith's editor, Anita D. Rehker; Terry Beauchamp for her transcription services; Mark Szymanski, who created the cover design; and Paula Godwin Coppel, who had the divine idea for the book and served as midwife of the editing process.

—Stephanie Stokes Oliver
Vice President of Publishing
Unity House

Foreword
Paula Godwin Coppel

When *The Secret* took off like wildfire last year, Unity followers watched in amazement. A fundamental principle taught by Unity for more than 118 years, in a brilliantly repackaged and newly marketed form, was creating a global sensation. Understandably, seeing *The Secret* soar as a best-selling book and blockbuster film spurred a mix of feelings among Unity followers, ranging from pride, excitement and awe to envy, denial and criticism.

But *The Secret* did something else as well: It lit a fire under us. It caused those of us in the Unity movement to take another look at the depth, meaning and value of our teachings in the context of today's pervasive search for spiritual meaning. Moreover, we realized that in too many ways our own movement has become a well-kept secret. No longer willing to sit on the sidelines, we were stirred to action. Fueling this newly lit fire were a passion and determination to communicate what Unity believes is the critical centerpiece of all spiritual discussions: our oneness with God and with one another.

This book is the result of that conviction unleashed. It is a collection of heartfelt beliefs, lessons and viewpoints from Unity ministers, licensed teachers, prayer associates, congregants, donors, employees, friends and supporters. All are aimed at helping today's spiritual seekers discover truths that can help them not only live more satisfying lives, but also experience a deeper connection with the Divine.

And so we thank you, Rhonda Byrne, for unveiling *The Secret* and thereby opening a door for our own light to shine through. Thank you for providing the impetus for us to remember and articulate who we are, what we believe and how it can make a difference in individual lives as well as in all humanity. We send these thoughts, prayers and lessons forth to join the voices of spiritual leaders everywhere who are sharing their gifts with an awakening world.

Preface
What Is Unity?

Unity is a worldwide movement of prayer, education and publishing that helps people of all faiths apply positive spiritual principles in their daily lives. At its heart, it is a positive, practical, progressive approach to Christianity. Founded in 1889 by Charles and Myrtle Fillmore, Unity teaches the effective, daily application of the principles of Truth as taught and exemplified by Jesus Christ. It encourages individuals to take personal responsibility to achieve greater health, love, prosperity, joy and peace in their own lives.

Although Unity considers Jesus Christ to be its Way Shower, the movement honors and respects all spiritual masters and faith traditions. Unity believes that all people are created with sacred worth, and seeks to be of service to anyone seeking spiritual growth and support, regardless of his or her chosen path. Unity ministries, programs and services strive to be free of discrimination on the basis of race, gender, age, creed, religion, national origin, ethnicity, physical disability and sexual orientation.

Unity has established about 900 centers of study and worship throughout the world where people discover and practice the Unity way of life. Physical, mental and emotional needs are addressed through affirmative prayer and spiritual education.

The Unity Secret

Charles R. Fillmore

Unity teaches us that there is a divine law of prosperity by means of which we can avail ourselves of the riches of the kingdom of heaven. By getting in rhythm with "the law of giving and receiving," as it is often called, we can demonstrate unlimited supply to meet all our needs. The secret is that we must learn to become open, receptive, responsive, and obedient to the law in order to make ourselves channels for the inflow and outflow of God's good.

Unity assures us that if just one person has learned the secret of successful living, then anyone can because "God is no respecter of persons" (Acts 10:34 KJV).

Excerpted from *The Adventure Called Unity* (2005) by Charles R. Fillmore, grandson of Unity founders Charles and Myrtle Fillmore.

Introduction

Daniel B. Rebant

Unity has been quietly teaching spiritual principles like the law of attraction for more than 118 years. In Unity, the law of attraction is more commonly called the law of mind action, and it is one of Unity's five basic principles.

In explaining the law of attraction in her book *The Secret,* Rhonda Byrne states, "What you think about the most or focus on the most will appear in your life." In Unity, the law of mind action states, "We are co-creators with God, creating our reality through thoughts held in mind." This is sometimes simplified as "Thoughts held in mind produce after their kind."

Thus, by whatever name, the principle is the same: What we think about most, supported by strong feelings and actions, eventually shows up in our lives. If we think positively, positive things will happen. If we think negatively, negative things will happen.

Our thoughts transmit magnetic energy at different frequencies. Whatever energy we send out through our thoughts will attract things at the same frequency. Like attracts like, so whatever we think about persistently and passionately will eventually create the reality we live in. To change our reality, we can begin by changing our thinking.

Negative thoughts—including fear, resentment, anger, despair and hatred—have low vibrations of energy. Positive thoughts of peace, gratitude, joy and love all transmit at much higher levels. Love sends forth the highest vibration of all. And as we transmit, so we receive. Loving thoughts create more love.

Unity co-founder Charles Fillmore explained it this way: "It is the law of Spirit that we must *be* that which we would draw to us. If we would draw to us love, we must *be* love, be loving and kind; if we would have peace and harmony in our environment, we must establish it within ourselves."

The Power of Love

Love is preeminent in the message of Jesus Christ. He knew its power to transform lives when he gave his followers a new commandment to "love one another" (Jn. 13:34 NRSV). This directive marked a quantum leap in consciousness for anyone willing and courageous enough to accept the challenge to love as Jesus did.

As the most powerful magnetic force in the universe, love draws more love to the one who gives it. Yet love's nature is not to receive, only to give. What a wonderful paradox! The more we give, the more we receive.

"If you are not attracting the good that you desire in your life, learn to express love; become a radiating center of love; and you will find that love, the divine magnet within you, will change your whole world," said May Rowland, former director of the Silent Unity prayer ministry.

Giving and Receiving

Spiritual principles are universally available. They are gifts from God. As with gravity or the very air we breathe, there is really nothing secret about these universal laws. Jesus taught them to everyone who was ready and willing to learn, regardless of their social, political or religious status. All the inspired masters throughout human history have done the same. Spiritual principles are the laws of the universe, available to anyone "with ears to hear" and "eyes to see."

Other spiritual principles deepen our understanding and application of the law of attraction. For example, the law of giving and receiving, when practiced with the law of attraction, adds amazing power to draw good into our lives. Jesus taught the law of giving and receiving when he said, "The measure you give will be the measure you get" (Mt. 7:2 NRSV).

The act of giving from the heart transcends material desires and human ego by accessing the sea of divine substance from which all blessings flow. It opens the channel for more good to flow into our lives. As St. Francis of Assisi said, "It is in giving that we receive."

So if you desire more money, begin by giving from what you have. If you desire more love from others, love others first. If you desire more fulfilling work, give your best to the job you have. If you desire more health, give from the health you have. Do this believing that God will provide what you long for, and you will receive more—much more than you ever imagined. "For it is your Father's good pleasure to give you the kingdom" (Lk. 12:32 NRSV).

Seek God First

Unity emphasizes the importance of aligning one's thoughts with the mind of God—of seeking God's will, not forcing our own. When we pray for the desires of our hearts, we affirm the highest good for ourselves and all others involved. To align with the highest perspective, we seek God first in everything.

Jesus taught, "Seek ye first the kingdom of God and his righteousness, and all these things shall be added unto you" (Mt. 6:33 KJV). In other words, align yourself completely with God Mind and everything you need in this world will flow your way.

Here are some approaches and resources for aligning yourself with the mind of God and, in so doing, placing yourself in the divine flow:

> 1. Live in an attitude of constant prayer, as Jesus did, to the point where you feel at one with your Source.

In the Master's own words, "The Father and I are one" (Jn. 10:30 NRSV). Through constant prayer, both alone and with others, he maintained this vital connection with God. And from this spiritual unity, Jesus demonstrated how to pray—first, by raising his vision above any human challenge to the all-providing realm of Spirit; by giving thanks in advance for the divine solution; and by affirming the spiritual Truth and receiving the answer. In Unity, we call this "affirmative prayer." To help maintain your attitude of prayer, Unity offers inspiration every day through *Daily Word®* magazine (1-800-669-0282, *www.unityonline.org, www.dailyword.com*). For special prayer support, you may contact the Silent Unity prayer ministry at anytime day or night (1-800-NOW-PRAY, *www.silentunity.org*).

> 2. Become part of a loving community of faith.

If you are not already part of a spiritual support group, you may consider joining one of the many vibrant

Unity churches and study groups around the world. One may be located near you (816-524-7414, *www.unity.org*). There is great power in the positive energy of groups like these, not only to help you grow spiritually and discover your unique gifts in service to others, but to bless the world. In fact, the entire Unity family joins together on the second Thursday of September every year for Unity World Day of Prayer. Please add your loving energy to ours as we send a great blessing to the earth and all its inhabitants (1-800-669-0282, *www.worlddayofprayer.org*).

3. Expand your spiritual understanding.

Unity offers classes, both online and on campus; spiritual retreats at beautiful Unity Village (1-866-34-UNITY, *www.spiritpathonline.org*); and a wide variety of books, CDs and other publications like *Daily Word* and *Unity Magazine*® to deepen your knowledge of spiritual principles and how to apply them in your life (1-800-779-0383, *www.unityonline.org*). Unity also offers free programs and discussion on its Internet radio network at *www.unity.fm*.

4. Be a spiritual activist.

Learning to love as Jesus did requires most of us to live more consciously and at greater depth. It requires living as "spiritual activists"—that is, as people who act from the deepest center of their beings, from a heart filled to overflowing with divine love.

As Rebecca Clark envisioned in her book *The Rainbow Connection*, "Wouldn't it be a glorious service for humanity to begin a chain of love, allowing it to flow from you, continuing to expand from one person to another until it quickly multiplied and magnified as a resounding force that would be felt throughout the universe?"

The positive energy of love is irresistible. It is God expressing through us and as us. Recognizing our oneness, we can link hearts and minds and know that our love and service will indeed change the world. And so it will be.

1.
Unity With God

The Source

CHARLOTTE SHELTON, ED.D.

*"As we align with the Source,
we access infinite power. Learning to tap
into this Source can lead to miraculous
changes in our individual lives
and in the lives of those around us."*

The foundational principle of Unity is the belief that there is only one power and presence in the universe, God, or infinite good. This differentiates Unity from the many other spiritual paths that espouse duality—good and evil. These other spiritual approaches are premised on the belief that humans are inherently sinful and must be "saved" from their evil nature, whereas Unity teaches that we are all manifestations of God, and as this Source is only good, we, who are made in the image and likeness of God, also are inherently good.

At first blush, many people find Unity's principle of innate goodness to be irrational. After all, we only have to turn on our televisions or pick up a newspaper to see a plethora of events that suggest evil is alive and well on planet Earth. We in Unity do not live with our heads in the sand. We don't deny that seemingly "bad" things happen, even to good people; but we do believe that people's "bad" behaviors are not driven by an evil power, but rather by an absence of awareness of who they really are ... children of God ... expressions of infinite goodness.

Light is a good example. Light is not the opposite of darkness. Rather, darkness is simply the result of blocked light. Light is always present in the physical universe, though we sometimes can't see it. Likewise, good is omnipresent, though the expression of good is sometimes blocked by the human ego. As we do our spiritual work, we discover our true nature and begin to claim our authentic identity as manifestations of good, children of the Source. We begin to live the Good life and see only Good in all that we experience. We discover that we are born into a world of original blessing, not one of original sin.

For those who believe that God is a person, a heavenly father sitting on a throne in the sky, this perspective may make little sense; but for those who are willing to explore new ways of thinking, new ways of defining God are possible—new ways that are more congruent with recent scientific thinking.

For example, quantum physicists believe the foundational substance of the universe is the quantum field. The physical world quite literally emerges from this invisible energy field. Physicists define this field as infinite, omnipresent and omnipotent. It sounds like a description of God. Perhaps this infinite energy source is synonymous with the infinite, omnipresent and omnipotent power of God Mind.

God as infinite energy is, in fact, congruent with both Eastern religions and mystical Christian traditions. When we redefine God as mind energy, we begin to shift our perceptions of who we are and what we are capable of becoming. We begin to sense that we are essentially energy beings, connected at the quantum level to the infinite energy Source.

Thus, we have amazing potential. We can, through mastery of the law of mind action, literally re-create our lives. As we begin to use this law, we discover that thoughts held in mind, do, indeed, create after their kind. We discover that as we align with the Source, we access infinite power. Learning to tap into this Source can lead to miraculous changes in our individual lives and in the lives of those around us.

Power, however, can be used in both constructive and destructive ways, as the atomic bomb so clearly demonstrates. The same principle that destroyed Hiroshima and Nagasaki lights cities and fuels rocket ships. The principle is the same, the human impact dramatically different. So as we begin to acknowledge our infinite power, which has recently been referred to as "The Secret," we also must acknowledge that this power can be used to advance humankind or further diminish the life of the human community. The power is the same. The application of this power depends on each of us.

Awakening to our potential, moving out of our sense of powerlessness and victimization, is the first step. Learning to transcend our human egos and make decisions that are good for the whole is a much more difficult second step. In order to do so, we must each commit to a path of spiritual transformation.

Though different spiritual traditions promote different transformational practices, all recognize the value of spending time daily in prayer and meditation. Unity's unique approach to prayer is called *affirmative prayer.* Rather than beseeching a reluctant God to grant the desires of our heart, affirmative prayer recognizes that in the Mind of God, our prayers are already answered. There is no lack at the power Source. Any experienced lack in our lives is a reflection of us, not of God. If God is infinite power, then infinite Good is ours for the claiming. We learn to claim our good through affirmative prayer, which changes our thinking (not God's).

If we are to fully connect to the Source, we not only spend time each day praying, we also spend time listening. Unity calls this *entering the Silence.* Practicing the Silence is similar to other meditative practices in that it is entering a state beyond words ... a place of deep connection to the Source ... a place not so much characterized by listening as by simply being.

I like to think of time in the Silence as my docking station. It is the time each day when I intentionally connect to the power Source that fuels my life and the workings of the entire universe. As I do so, I transcend my little self, my ego self, and merge with a greater power, a higher power, that not only changes how I see myself, it shifts my perception of the external world. From this place of greater insight, I not only see the world differently, I act differently. My limited, fear-based thinking is transformed (my brain wave and heart

wave patterns literally change) and, consequently, I am able
to make choices that not only serve my highest good; they
serve the good of the whole.

Where to begin? How does one silence the "monkey
brain," as the Buddhists like to call the ceaseless propensity
for thinking that permeates our waking hours? How does
one learn to enter a state of Silence? We learn to meditate in
the same way we learn any other new skill … by practicing.
While teachers, books or CDs may provide useful guidance,
ultimately we learn to quiet our brain by learning to surrender to the knowing of the heart. And, in so doing, we discover the mythical point that Archimedes was looking for—a
place to stand and move the world. We've always had such a
place available to us, and we always will. It has been inside
us all along. It is activated as we recognize who and what we
really are—manifestations of infinite energy, unlimited beings
of Light!

So in this era of enthusiasm about "The Secret," I want
to go on record as advocating for an awareness of the Source.
Simply understanding "The Secret" without understanding
the Source is not likely to eradicate all that challenges the sus-
tainability of life on our planet. Yes, using "The Secret" can
enable us to manifest our heart's desires … our material heart's
desires; however, connecting to the Source enables us to satisfy
the desire of our souls for connection—with the Divine and
with each other. And, it is this awareness of our deep intercon-
nectivity that enables us to transcend our individual needs and
choose actions that serve us all.

I affirm that you will claim your infinite power and
that you will use this power not only for material good, but

for service to the greater good. Jesus' teachings remind us that we are our brothers' and sisters' keeper. A quantum physicist would suggest that we are actually intertwined with our brothers and sisters and with the physical universe. Our atoms are continuously recycled with everyone and everything around us, living or not. Paramhansa Yogananda wrote: "We are a drop in the ocean; whatever happens to the ocean happens to the drop, whatever happens to the drop happens to the ocean." We are all one ... we are Unity!

Co-creators With God

MANZEL BERLIN

*"Prayers are powerful not because
we change the mind of a stingy God
or because we magically manipulate secret laws
of the universe, but because we are in tune
with the divine truth."*

The universe operates according to spiritual as well as physical laws. Thoughts are powerful. Not only do our actions help to shape our world, but our very thoughts strongly influence the physical world.

Yet it would be a great mistake to think we each create our own separate world. Quantum physics tells us that the notion of separate and isolated particles is false. Separation is an illusion. Reality is, instead, holistic. Even seeming chaos has an order and design which can be detected. Seemingly unrelated events have an impact on each other: a butterfly fluttering its wings in China does have some influence on the weather in Kansas. If new science prompts new metaphysics, then one of the most important conclusions is that we are not sovereign creators of our own separate and isolated little worlds.

The truth is, we are co-creators with God. We each create in concert with the divine within us, like having dual controls. Reality is far more malleable than previously imagined. It is not fixed, static and beyond our creative reach. Reality is ever-changing through our co-creation with God.

Our thoughts do attract people, things and events into our lives. However, this does not mean we should blame ourselves for everything that goes wrong. Such blaming is sometimes referred to as *metaphysical malpractice.*

The truth is that we are free to choose how we respond to every situation in life. No situation is beyond divine blessing; no matter how tragic the event, it is not beyond our blessing and not beyond God's blessing. The creation process continues as we emerge from each occurrence. There is one presence and one power active in the universe and in our lives. That divine power is God, the good, which exists within us and among us.

Knowing spiritual laws does not make us magicians who can manipulate the universe to serve our selfish wishes. Rather, when we understand our power as co-creators, shaping our world with our thoughts, prayers, words and actions, we open ourselves to live more fully. Jesus said, "I have come that you might have life and have it abundantly." Abundant life is one of the gifts we receive when we are in tune with divine spirit. But abundance does not mean excess. We are in error thought if we use abundance as an excuse to hoard or waste precious resources, neglect our fellow creatures or abuse planet earth. The law of attraction is not our own private genie in a bottle. It is but one small aspect of the power of love. Love is the greatest power in the universe, and whatever we do for selfish or malicious purposes is not love.

Metaphysics is not magic; it is the study of universal truth. When we are in tune with universal truth, we are empowered in that beautiful way Jesus described: "You shall know the truth and the truth shall make you free." No book, religion or denomination has a copyright on truth, and neither do we as individuals. Reality is holographic. Everything in the hologram reflects the whole truth. Nothing in the hologram is able to separate itself; everything and everyone is connected. A life lived attuned to the infinite is truly abundant and truly powerful.

Unity co-founder Myrtle Fillmore also knew the liberating power of truth. Thousands of people turned to Myrtle for her love, her wisdom, for healing and for the magnificent prayer ministry she launched called Silent Unity. Prayer workers were often delighted when people reported that they had experienced healing. Myrtle cautioned the prayer workers to never think that it was their own power that effected the healing but that it was in being in tune with the divine power that they were able to participate in that healing which was always God's work. Prayers are powerful not because we change the mind of a stingy God or because we magically manipulate secret laws of the universe, but because we are in tune with the divine truth. Myrtle believed that her own healing was a manifestation of this principle. Her prayers were not magic incantations; they were affirmations of truth. They were not the power of positive thinking or evidence of strong will; they were prayers of alignment with divine truth.

Our egos like to imagine that we are great wizards. But that is not true power. True power is being connected to the supreme source. It is not creating our own little world with our positive thoughts—it is by knowing and aligning with truth that we are empowered and truly set free!

Demonstrating God: More Than Just Talk

Rev. Gregory C. Guice

"When we seek to demonstrate the will of God, we are bringing into manifestation a Divine energy that attracts to us the abundance and substance needed for a greater expression of God in our lives."

We've all read dozens of books and engaged in countless discussions about what we desire, yet how many of us are actually demonstrating, or manifesting, our dreams? Many of us are still searching for ways and ideas to draw to us our life dreams, our personal wealth, a new love, and the list goes on.

Our quest is well founded. Within each of us is that innate desire, the presence of life that cries from within us: The "I AM."

This is the hidden ingredient that fuels the law of attraction. If our desire is to bring our longings into manifestation,

we must look within and realize we need more than just a
verbal discourse on the intellectual and mental encampment
of thought. If we are to move into the realm of manifestation,
we must actually become the words we study and the vibration we hope to attract. Our goal and desire should be to
demonstrate the law of attraction by bringing into manifestation that which we know as God.

   According to Webster, the word *demonstrate* means:
"To prove by reasoning, as by deduction; to establish as true."
In our search for the meaning of life, we find ourselves exam-
ining our own Truth according to what we are attracting in or
manifesting in our life. The process of attraction and manifestation is achieved in direct proportion to our ability to demonstrate the teachings and principles of Jesus Christ.

   According to Unity co-founder Charles Fillmore,
to demonstrate Truth "is to effect a change of consciousness. This includes the elimination of error and establish-
ment of Truth." Many of us are still held in bondage by our
own wounded and erroneous thoughts and the sometimes
unconscious enslavement to lack thinking and feelings of
unworthiness. Many individuals talk about wanting to create
more prosperity in their lives or wanting to attend college to
achieve a dream of becoming a doctor, lawyer, teacher, etc.
They start off on their quest with the right intention; however, the moment the first storm arises in their journey, they
begin to melt under self-generated fears. They say things
like, "I can't; they won't let me; I don't have enough money"
and before long, their song is a melody of victimization.
They become like the disciples of Jesus who found themselves at sea when a great storm arose with heavy winds and

waves pounding against their ship. Finally the disciples cried out to Jesus who was asleep in the boat. With their fears written all over their faces, the disciples woke Jesus and said to him, "Master, carest thou not that we perish?" Arising from his sleep, Jesus rebuked the wind and said unto the sea, "Peace, be still."

This story illustrates how many of us are impaired in our ability to demonstrate: We let our fears rage within us, blocking our ability to trust the presence of God. We cry out to the Lord, to our inner Christ presence, seeking to be rescued from the storms of life, unaware that our fears are unreal messengers of thought. They have no power and no presence unless we give them dominion. It is a metaphysical law that whatever thoughts we hold in our minds are attracted to us and then brought into our consciousness for manifestation. We become the instruments for manifesting and demonstrating our truth. When we want to demonstrate spiritual principles, or the teachings of Jesus Christ, we must have a conscious awareness that is centered on the intended spiritual demonstration. In Unity we express this demonstration as "The proving of a Truth principle in one's body or affairs. The manifestation of an ideal when its accomplishment has been brought about by one's conformity in thought, words and action to the creative Principle of God."

A sense of oneness with God becomes our desired vibration. This vibration is the power of prayer created by a prayerful consciousness that acknowledges the active presence of the Christ in every demonstration and every manifestation.

God's will for us is to demonstrate in our lives the universal laws and Truth principles that preside over this entire universe, over every living creature, every thought

and every cell of our being. When we seek to demonstrate
the will of God, we are bringing into manifestation a Divine
energy that attracts to us the abundance and substance
needed for a greater expression of God in our lives.

Prayer is a demonstration and expression of our gratitude to God for all the goodness and glory that is constantly
being poured into our lives. When we pray, we are in com-
munion with God, thus bridging and activating the law of
mind action. Scripture says, "Seek ye first the kingdom of
God, and his righteousness; and all these things shall be added
unto you" (Mt. 6:33 KJV). As we seek to demonstrate God's
will, we are releasing our personal will and allowing God's will
to be done in our lives. We begin by discerning in spirit what
God's will is for us. We do not seek to demonstrate God for
any material want, need or desire for ourselves.

In Joel Goldsmith's book *Practicing the Presence*, he
asks, "What are we seeking? Is it God that we are seeking,
or are we seeking something from God? Are we seeking a
realization of God, or are we trying to reach God in order
to get something through God?" The questions that Joel
Goldsmith raises help us understand what it means to demonstrate God. Goldsmith writes, "We must demonstrate
God—not persons, things or conditions." He further says,
"Our entire demonstration must be the realization of God,
the demonstration of God, the consciousness of God's presence." Consciousness becomes the vehicle for demonstrating God.

Each and every day, we have the opportunity to
awaken a new awareness of Christ, to begin our lives filled
with an inner presence and knowledge of the Holy Spirit. If

you truly want to demonstrate God in your life, open yourself to these few ideas:

- Recognize God as the preeminent principle and Presence in all creation.
- Become still and go to that sacred place within.
- Enter into a consciousness of gratitude and thanksgiving.
- Acknowledge God's will as your will and release any other thought.
- Seek only the Kingdom of Heaven, and the Christ within.

"Shew me thy ways, O Lord; teach me thy paths. Lead me in thy truth, and teach me; for thou art the God of my salvation; on thee do I wait all the day" (Ps. 25:4-5 KJV).

To demonstrate God, we must simply remember that it is more than just talk: It is God.

EGO = Edging God Out

REV. ELLEN DEBENPORT

> *"It took years of self-reflection and spiritual study
> to learn that I was laboring under a mistaken
> impression of who I truly am—my true Self.
> I am a spiritual being having a human experience."*

A provocative question has arisen about the law of attraction and the idea that our thoughts and feelings create our experience: If we believe that we create our own reality, where is God?

How presumptuous, some might say, to imply that we are in charge! Isn't that just running rampant with our egos, thinking we can control everything, when in fact we should be seeking God's will? Who are we to see ourselves as creators of our own experience? Shouldn't we turn to God for guidance rather than ourselves?

I struggled with these questions years ago, and I still hear them frequently from people just learning about the

law of attraction. One man said that trying to understand
that he attracts everything into his own life has been a "God-
shattering experience."

I remember that feeling. When I first heard the idea
that I was a co-creator with God, it sounded grandiose and
blasphemous. I was being encouraged to relocate God as
being *within me* instead of *out there* watching and tending
to my needs. But that made me feel I was praying to myself,
which seemed wrong! And when ministers and teachers told
me I had all the answers within, I felt bereft. Obviously, I
thought, if I had the answers, I would be using them.

It took years of self-reflection and spiritual study to
learn that I was laboring under a mistaken impression of
who I truly am—my true Self. I am a spiritual being having a
human experience. I am an expression of God on earth. I am
divine at my essence, my core, and I am never separate from
God. As Jesus said, the Father and I are one.

That means I have access to infinite divine wisdom,
guidance, love and strength, like a desktop computer tapped
into the Internet. I have a higher self or inner being—my
God-connection—that knows exactly what I need and draws
it to me. I simply set an intention, and the universe rushes to
support me.

Practicing the law of attraction means consciously
and deliberately using our thoughts and feelings to bring
more abundance into our lives. It may be love, health,
strength, prosperity or anything else, but it all comes from
God. It all originates in invisible substance and is brought
into form through our thinking. It already has been provided
for us as part of Creation.

We are made in God's image, and God is nothing if not creative, so we are creators too. What an amazing aspect of Creation that we can draw anything into our lives with our thinking! What we hold in our hearts and minds appears in our reality. I have come to believe that we are never more spiritual, never more in touch with God, than when we are co-creating our lives with the Divine. It is exactly what we came to earth to do.

The Good Life: Created, Not Acquired

LILA HERRMANN

*"The Truth of our existence is not
some random chain of events or chaotic emotions;
it is the reflection of our choices."*

The law of attraction provides an unshakable foundation for creating the life we truly desire. The law of attraction—defined by Unity cofounder Charles Fillmore as "the law that all conditions and circumstances in affairs and body are attracted to us to accord with the thoughts we hold steadily in consciousness"—has implications far beyond the limited scope of material gain. It is really about accumulating a whole, healthy, balanced, substantial and meaningful life. The law of attraction is not about getting, it's about living.

In the Gospel of Mark (11:24) it is said, "All things ye pray and ask for, believe that ye receive them, and ye shall have them." This idea of abundance and having our desires met is not new. What is new for some, however, is the realization that what we want is already here, waiting for us—it may not be in the shape or form we wanted or expected, but "it is God's good pleasure to give us the kingdom." That doesn't mean there's a mercurial, human-like God, sometimes saying yes and sometimes saying no, like a spiritual version of *Deal or No Deal*. It means God is working through us to bring forth our highest good. And we have a role to play too. We must open our hearts and minds to accept the good that is ours. God is our Source, and to receive our good, we must let go and let God ... let God's will be done, through us.

I etting go does not mean sacrificing all that we want or think we need in the material world. We aren't taking a vow of poverty or shunning physical comfort or refusing to enjoy anything that isn't sacred or spiritual. In his book *Discover the Power Within You*, the late Unity minister Eric Butterworth took issue with the belief that poverty is a virtue and that it is a Christian duty to be poor. Butterworth asserted that Jesus implied it was actually a sin to be poor, indicating "if you are experiencing lack, you are not accepting yourself in the fullness of your own unique relationship with the Infinite." Butterworth said the lesson to be learned from the stories of miracles in the Bible is that the universe is "opulent, limitless, and accommodating. It will manifest for us exactly what we have the consciousness to encompass." This is where our responsibility comes into play. According to Unity principle, "We are co-creators with God, creating reality through thoughts held in mind."

What we think about, how we act, where we place focus, all determine our reality. *Like attracts like.* As Charles Fillmore said, "If we would draw to us love, we must be love, be loving and kind; if we would have peace and harmony in our environment, we must establish it within ourselves." When we become consciously aware of our wholeness and perfect well-being, it will be manifested physically. When we know the Truth—that God has blessed us with prosperity and abundance—our wealth will appreciate. When we serve as peacemakers, we will know serenity in our own hearts. Seek ye the kingdom of God and his righteousness, says Matthew 6:33, and all these things will be given to you as well.

As human beings, we tend to be ruled by our emotions. We believe that what we feel is out of our control and we must just accept it. But the Truth of our existence is not some random chain of events or chaotic emotions; it is the reflection of our choices. We create our own reality. With our consciousness, we create a life.

In his book *Prosperity*, Charles Fillmore states, "The words of your mouth and the thoughts of your heart are now and always molding the spiritual substance and bringing it into manifestation." By practicing the law of attraction, we can draw to us what we truly want and need. We can draw to us what fulfills us—spiritually, intellectually and physically. There is balance and substance and meaning. Will there be abundance and prosperity? Yes, but also the true riches of mindfulness, serenity, love, faith and creativity.

Myrtle Fillmore said, "Prosperity is not an accumulation of money or other so-called wealth.... Wouldn't you dread to think that men and women were always to be deluded with the belief that ... formed things are the realities, the truly valuable things of life?" She added, "True prosperity is not making money, or putting out goods, or developing property. It is determining what our own individual soul requires in order to cause it to unfold more and more of God."

The law of attraction is not a secret code, but a key— the key to a life of fulfillment, wholeness and well-being. Through the law of attraction, we become active participants, co-creating with God the life we desire. God's gifts for us are here and now; it is up to us to open up to receive them.

The Secret Is in the Silence

REV. ELEANOR FLEMING, PH.D.

"A solution requires a new state of consciousness, fed by a conscious connection with the source, which results from a disciplined daily practice in the silence."

The word *secret* has the same root as the word *sacred*. Jesus knew that anything that is sacred is kept inside.

In the Sermon on the Mount (Mt. 6:6 Lamsa Bible), Jesus instructs us to "go into your inner chamber and lock the door, and pray to your Father who is in secret, and your Father who sees in secret shall himself reward you openly ... for your Father knows what you need, before you ask him." That inner chamber is also referred to as the Secret Place of the Most High. Why? It is a sacred place where we know God.

The real secret is that the power and presence of God, the Source of our Good, the Kingdom of God, are within us.

Unity founders Charles and Myrtle Fillmore lived the Truth that Jesus taught. They wrote a covenant, dedicating all of their resources to the Spirit of Truth—not to acquire anything in return but knowing they would be provided whatever they needed to accomplish their work. I am filled with awe when I think of Myrtle and Charles Fillmore, two ordinary people with health problems, who built the Unity movement on the Truth that they were spiritual beings and had free and open access to the infinite source of Good. On the cornerstone of the building of the original world headquarters at Ninth and Tracy in Kansas City, Missouri, is this scripture: "Built upon the foundation of the apostles and prophets, Jesus Christ himself being the cornerstone ..." In the language of the soul this means that the cornerstone of the building is built upon the Christ consciousness, "in whom the whole structure is joined together and grows into a holy temple in the Lord" (Eph. 2:21 RSV).

Having served as the associate minister now for four years at Unity Church Universal, the church that the Fillmores founded, I am very aware of the roots of Unity and of the healing work that went on there. Many people knew that Myrtle Fillmore healed herself of tuberculosis, but few are aware that her ministry was like that of Jesus, healing the lame, the deaf, the blind. A Unity article quoted *The Kansas City Star*, stating that Unity Church Universal was the "greatest healing center in the world." Hundreds of people lined the halls waiting for appointments with Myrtle and her practitioners. After the Silent Unity Prayer Practitioners moved

next door to 917 Tracy Avenue, Myrtle Fillmore maintained
her office in the original building so she could continue to
meet one-on-one with those who sought spiritual healing.
The Fillmores' inspiring lessons in Truth resulted in standing-
room-only Sunday services. The Fillmores were not striving
for material success; they simply lived the Truth that Jesus
taught, and their consciousness attracted success to them.

What has been done once can be done again. Each of
us has that same ability. We are made in the image and likeness of God, and we have the same access to Truth principles
as spiritual leaders such as the Fillmores. The question is,
Do we have the same level of faith and courage to risk all our
inner and outer resources in demonstrating that Truth?

This question led me to form New Foundation Unity,
a traveling educational ministry with a curriculum designed
to help people reconnect with the roots of Unity. I considered
the elements of power and substance that shaped success
in the early Unity years. The foundation was the practice of
prayer in the silence. Charles and Myrtle spent many hours
in silence, consciously connecting with the sacred source.
People who want to make changes in their lives, their busi-
nesses, their churches, often forget that the consciousness
that created the problems can never be the consciousness
that solves them. A solution requires a new state of consciousness, fed by a conscious connection with the source,
which results from a disciplined daily practice in the silence.
Time in the silence is sacred. We must learn to place it ahead
of everything else in our lives until it becomes such a part of
our functioning that it has more authority over our thinking,
our words and our actions than the outer voices of the world.

As the late Unity minister Eric Butterworth said, we must create the conditions in consciousness that make the results inevitable. There are no substitutes or shortcuts if we want lasting results.

The second element in the Fillmores' spiritual practice was the metaphysical study of the Bible. They understood the Bible to be a record of spiritual experience that provided invaluable insight into our own spiritual experiences. The language of the soul is beyond the physical world, and we must be fluent in this metaphysical language in order to develop an understanding faith.

The third element of the Fillmores' practice was healing. *Healing, holy* and *wholeness* all stem from the same root word. Healing is more than removing physical symptoms. Healing means bringing into full expression the wholeness of our essential nature. Our spiritual journey into wholeness brings forth our spiritual power in service to the world, so we can do the "greater works" that Jesus promised.

Truth is eternal. We learn about Truth in our sacred times of prayer. Together we can do greater works by rebuilding our foundation in consciousness through a daily practice of prayer, quiet reflection and service, so that heaven can truly be manifest on earth.

2.
Exploring the Law of Attraction

Your Thought
Is Your Life

*"To make the law of attraction work for you,
you must pay attention to three things:
your thoughts, your feelings and the way
you respond to opportunities."*

In 1959 Unity first published Charles Fillmore's *The Revealing Word*, which included definitions of every metaphysical term he had encountered in his 60-year study of metaphysics. For the *law of attraction* he wrote: "The law that all conditions and circumstances in (our) affairs and body are attracted to us in accord with the thoughts we hold steadily in consciousness."

So how is this attraction possible? It's based on the fact that everything in the universe is energy. We are mass energy. Yes, we have a body and yes, we are spirit, and all

of that is energy in different forms. We send energy forth
from our consciousness that is directed by our thoughts, our
words and our actions. Like the signal from a radio or television station, our energy is not visible, so we live our lives
unaware of the power that resides within and around us. But
we transmit this energy like ripples on a pond, with every
thought we think and every word we speak.

The Gospel of John begins with, "In the beginning was
the Word, and the Word was with God, and the Word was
God ... and the Word was made flesh." We have interpreted
this passage to symbolize the physical manifestation of Jesus as
the Son of God, but could this message also be telling us that
the Word made flesh is the God-energy that moves through all
of us in the thoughts we think and words we use? If so, *this* is
the energy that determines the results that unfold in our lives.

As an example: A woman named Betty was reared by
a mean-spirited stepmother who betrayed her repeatedly, both
physically and emotionally. As a result, Betty harbored resentment
and anger long after she grew up, which held her back from experiencing any kind of a fulfilling life ... until she realized she had
given her power to her stepmother years after she moved away.
When Betty accepted that the only power that she wanted in her
life was God's *loving* presence and God's good, she was able to
release thoughts of anger and replace them with thoughts of love
and forgiveness and blessings. She finally got it that *she* had been
hurting herself with her thoughts, not her stepmother. So, with
a new perspective, her life took on a new direction, her outlook
became one of joyful expectation, and suddenly opportunities
opened for her that had been closed for years.

Change your life? Change your thoughts!

Proverbs states: "As a man thinketh in his heart, so is he" (Prov. 23:7 KJV). Do you spend your time thinking about what you don't have, wishing for something better? Lots of people do. Or do you place your energy on thoughts of appreciation for all the good you are experiencing already?

People with repeated health challenges think and talk about all the things they can't do, and the result is an outpouring of negative energy that creates more of the same. It restricts the inflow of radiant health. One woman's constant fear has been of disease, illness and disability. Her conversations with neighbors and friends are limited to her doctor visits, her medications and the probability of impending surgery. She is also worried that her insurance won't cover the condition or won't last long enough for her to recover. It's no surprise that she sees her doctors several times a month, spends enormous sums on prescriptions, and has major or minor surgeries nearly every year. Is she really that sick, or have her thoughts and words become a self-fulfilling prophecy?

Because like attracts like and our dominant thoughts create our reality, her situation is not likely to change without a conscious decision to change her thoughts and words.

Taking time to go apart and get still, to meditate and relax in a state of positive expectation, can work wonders.

Another woman who lay in a hospital with an "incurable disease" had the whole situation reversed when an enlightened friend pointed out a scab that had formed over a cut. The friend said that the doctors and the medicine and the hospital couldn't form the scab, only the regenerative power she had within her could perform that miracle. And if God gave her that ability naturally, imagine the healing power God could provide, especially when amplified through prayer. With a whole new perspective, the woman began giving thanks for the healing taking place within her body every moment. A month later she walked out of the hospital without a trace of the disease.

There is a gravitational pull that keeps the universe in order. Everything in the universe is made of energy. Solids, liquids and gasses—everything is energy, including human cells. Every part of every atom and molecule is pure energy. Similar energies are attracted to one another in a "birds of a feather" kind of way, and discordant energies are pushed apart like an outgoing tide. The order of the universe depends on the bonding of similar energies and the disconnection of opposing ones. Our thoughts go out as energy waves and attract conditions and circumstances to us that have a similar energy frequency.

A statement in the Gospels demonstrates that Jesus was aware of the attraction and repulsion of energies, but it is not often quoted because on the surface it's misunderstood and seems unfair. "For to him who has will more be given, and he will have abundance; but from him who has not, even what he has will be taken away" (Mt. 13:12 RSV). This simply means that a person filled with love will attract loving people into his or her life: abundant friendships, intimate relationships and a joyful life experience. But what happens to a person who is hard-hearted, resentful, angry or jealous? Friendships disappear, relationships dissolve, and life can become very lonely.

Similarly, the person whose thoughts and words are focused only on sickness and ill health will attract an abundance of more sickness and poorer health. That is how the law of attraction works.

Many people say, Well, if that's true, why do I think about something and *not* get it? They might say, I think about a good and loving relationship, a good paying job, winning the lottery, and a slender, healthy body, but I'm not getting those things! The answer is simple; there's something inside that is in conflict with their desires.

You are the sum of all your life experiences. Old recordings stored in your subconscious may be keeping you from your actually believing you can have the relationship, the job, the winnings or the healthy body you desire. "I'm not good enough; I don't have the proper education or experience; I've never been successful with diet or exercise," and so on. These are old messages you've told yourself through the years, criticisms you've internalized from parents or teachers, or your own reflections on lack of previous success. They combine to nullify the energy that is going out to help you achieve your current desires.

The law of attraction is a wonderful law and it works for everyone, all the time. It attracts people, places and things to help you fulfill your dreams. It also brings challenges and struggles.

To make the law of attraction work for you, you must pay attention to three things: your thoughts, your feelings and the way you respond to opportunities.

Become a self-observer and allow yourself to become aware of your thoughts and words. Begin to understand how your own negative energies attract negative circumstances just as your positive energies attract good experiences. Then make a conscious choice to replace the negative thoughts and words with helpful, positive ones. You can do this easily by looking at every situation with eyes of gratitude, being grateful even for your challenges, for they present opportunities to learn, grow and rise above circumstances. Be grateful for all the blessings you receive, even the simple blessings of a beautiful morning, or the wonder of the telephone you use to call a friend.

A man named Robert was in a heavy state of debt. He was extremely stressed, with all his energies focused on putting off his creditors. The result? He continued to attract even more debt. Finally, recognizing that he had to break the cycle, he took time to objectively look at his problem and find a solution.

First he went to a beautiful park where he could clear his mind, get quiet and tune in to his inner voice for guidance. He realized that he had much to be grateful for, including the ability to address his problem without guilt or blame. Relaxed and inspired by the serenity of the park, his mind went to work and within a half hour, he had calculated a solution, written down a plan, made a list of the people to contact, and resolved to follow through immediately. In less than a week, by doing what was his to do, he had the problem under control.

Robert overcame his adversity by applying the law of attraction. His negative thoughts and feelings had been causing negative results—his debt. Through self-observation and a conscious switch to an attitude of gratitude, he sent new energy into the universe. Spirit directed this energy back to him in the form of a plan for a solution—a list of people who would support him in overcoming his financial problems and an opportunity to meet his creditors to gain their approval. Then he took appropriate action.

We get what we think about, we get what we talk about, we get what we feel in our guts, whether it's good or bad. Our life experiences are the result of whatever is going on in our minds or coming out of our mouths. Life does not happen *to* us, it happens *through* us.

The Secrets of Prosperity

REV. LORI FLEMING

> *"We will never get what we want until we ask for it, believing that we have already received it."*

Life is meant to be abundant in every area, including our spirituality, our relationships, our health and our finances. What is prosperity exactly? Is it more love, more stuff, more money? Prosperity is more than money—it is loving relationships; fulfillment in our employment; it is peace and serenity; it is an active spiritual life. We are the co-creators of our lives. We create everything by first having an idea, then doing whatever steps are necessary to bring that idea into fruition.

Jesus taught us to ask, seek and knock. Wayne Dyer, in *The Power of Intention*, recommends something called "thinking from the end," a process of visualizing what we want, holding that mind picture in our consciousness, and doing everything necessary to make it happen. Whatever we can visualize, we can materialize. The creative process turns fantasy into fact.

Clarity is important. Most of the time, we are not specific about what we want. What if, instead, we were to expect our desire to show up in the same way we order something from a catalog or online? Then we would believe it will appear on the doorstep in a few days. When we believe it will happen, when we see it as already ours, it rapidly comes into manifestation. It can also help to write down what we want; make a treasure map with colorful pictures and bold print. We can put it where it is visible every day and include a date by which it is to be achieved. Then, be grateful and bless this goal. Gratitude is just like plugging in the electricity to make an appliance work.

Before something we desire becomes manifest, before we accomplish our goal, we "fake it until we make it." Or we might say, "Act until it is fact." The universe will start to rearrange itself to make it happen for us with ease and grace. We do not have to know how it will happen—just have faith in the invisible, in the unseen. Everything we need to do will be shown to us along the way. We can follow that spiritual intuition, those feelings and knowings. They are from the Universal Mind of God, guiding us to the right and perfect outcome. We use our mind to access the ideas in Universal Mind as we think things into being. Buddha said, "All that we are is a result of what we have thought." In Matthew 21:22, Jesus says, "Whatever you ask for in prayer with faith, you will receive." We will never get what we want until we ask for it, believing that we have already received it.

We can consciously choose to have a pleasant day. We can choose to have a good experience when we take our car in for repair, affirming that the experience will be easy, quick and inexpensive.

When we rush or hurry, it brings up fear, which attracts more rush or hurry. If we say we don't have enough time, we are right. If we say we have plenty of time to do everything easily and efficiently, we will also be right.

If we want a different car, we go out and test-drive a new car. When we want a new sofa, we go to the furniture store, sit on a few sofas, feel the upholstery or leather, and visualize what it will look like in our home. If we want to take a trip, we get some travel brochures and hang them where we can see them every day. We can even add pictures of ourselves. In our minds, we feel what it would be like to be on that beach, that Paris street, or that cruise ship. How long will it take to manifest? As long as it takes for us to truly believe it will happen. Nothing is too big to accomplish. It is no harder to manifest something big than something small. It takes no effort for the universe to line up everything needed to meet our desire. The process is the same whether we are manifesting a stick of gum or a beach house.

To attract the right relationship, we can first focus on being the perfect partner. We can start noticing when we interact well with other people and tell ourselves what a good job we did in that interaction. We can practice feeling love and compassion for everyone and everything, being grateful for our friends. We can imagine what our perfect mate might look like, how he or she might act. We can even visualize the details of a day spent with this person, perhaps having a leisurely breakfast or taking a walk. This kind of visualization makes us feel joyous and alive. Time stops. We will then create in the outer exactly what we have imagined in the inner.

To attract money, we can focus on wealth, not on how much we have now. We cannot attract real wealth if we are focusing on lack. When we focus on not having enough, that is what we will get. When we "need" money, it creates a greater need of money, not more money. All the money we need is available right now. There is no lack. The universe is abundant. If we do not have enough, it is because we are blocking it through negative thinking. We can begin to listen to these thoughts, and if they are negative, turn them into positives. We can pay bills with gratitude—be grateful for the electric company for providing electricity, lights and air conditioning. We can visualize checks coming in the mail every time we go to the mailbox. Then, keep a record of how much comes in. The more we notice it and are grateful, the more we will get.

If our work becomes play, we will become prosperous. My friend Sandy Roth is a workshop facilitator. She wrote, "Make your values and purpose so clear that your work is a reminder of what you like best about yourself." I keep this above my desk, where I can see it every day.

I was raised to believe that you had to work hard for money and that money did not grow on trees. Now I'm replacing those negative beliefs with the affirmation that prosperity comes easily to me from many sources. And it does. I use affirmations such as: *I am a money magnet ... I have more than enough ... I am receiving money every day ... The universe is abundant ...* and I never forget to say thank you.

It is common knowledge that the wealthiest people on the planet give away large quantities of money. The universe responds to these philanthropists, returning enormous amounts of money and good back to them. We must first give money to get money. When we think we do not have enough, it is time to start giving. We can give of our time. Give of our talent and energy. Give of our financial resources. As we demonstrate faith in giving, the universe will respond in kind. Give with gratitude and love, not with doubt, dread or sacrifice. Giving from a heart filled with gratitude is one of the most powerful magnets in the universe. When we radiate joy from within and transmit that into the universe, we will experience true abundance.

Attitude = 100%

Rev. Sandra Rae Hymel

"It doesn't matter how the experience comes to you; you are in charge of your attitude toward it."

If it is true that we draw to us all of our experiences, this implies that we attract the painful, as well as the joyful, experiences. Or, as stated in Job 4:14: "That which I feared has come upon me."

Does this mean, then, that a child born with deformities has attracted this reality? Or that starving people in our world drew to them starvation? Does it mean people tortured in the holocaust, killed in 9/11, or victimized by hurricane Katrina attracted these atrocities? We err grievously when we oversimplify in this way.

Too often we hear a well-meaning spiritual practitioner chiding someone who is facing difficulty by saying, "What is it in your consciousness that drew this issue to you?"

Such an application of the law of attraction is what I call "New Age sin"—the erroneous application of a basic truth. The story told in John 9:1-3 illustrates why: "As he (Jesus) went along he saw a man blind from birth. His disciples asked him, 'Rabbi, who sinned, this man or his parents, that he was born blind?' 'Neither this man nor his parents sinned,' Jesus answered, 'but that happened so that the work of God might be manifested in his life.'" In other words, this turn of events occurred to open the way for a greater manifestation of God.

At the heart of adversity lies opportunity—the opportunity to choose an attitude that demonstrates the Christ-power in each of us. This Christ-power stems from our faith in God active in the heart of all humankind.

Wars, earthquakes, famines, the passing of loved ones, even the downsizing of jobs are very much part of our life experience. The critical question is, What is our attitude in the midst of these experiences? Do we choose to *grow* through them or just *go* through them? Jesus said, "Such things must happen … yet see to it that you are not alarmed … for all these things are but the beginning of birth pains" (Mt. 24:6-8). In other words, there is nothing to fear, for God is here! God, the good, is forever present and always creating new beginnings from seeming chaos.

In the face of any challenge, we can ask, What is my attitude toward this person or experience? At any given moment, we can choose an experience of heaven or hell. "For as a man thinks within himself, so is he" (Prov. 23:7).

We might say that attitude = 100 percent! That is, your attitude toward each of life's experiences determines 100 percent of the reward you reap. In fact, if you add together the numerical position in the alphabet of each letter in the word *attitude*, the numbers equal 100!

A – 1
T – 20
T – 20
I – 9
T – 20
U – 21
D – 4
E – 5
100

Some of the most powerful stories of the importance of attitude have been told by survivors of the Nazi concentration camps. In Viktor E. Frankl's inspiring book *Man's Search for Meaning*, he writes: "We who lived in concentration camps can remember the men who walked through the huts comforting others, giving away their last piece of bread. They may have been few in number, but they offer sufficient proof that everything can be taken from a man but one thing: the last of the human freedoms—to choose one's attitude in any given set of circumstances, to choose one's own way."

Unity co-founder Myrtle Fillmore advised many who came to her for prayer to "count it all joy." She saw problems as the gateway to growth. She once wrote to a Truth student, "Count it all joy—all those personal disappointments in people, even Truth students, because they have given you the impetus to rely upon your indwelling Lord." She also wrote, "When one door closes another opens, because God always opens new avenues of blessings when former conditions pass away." And finally, "The trials of today are stepping-stones over which you pass to a glorious destiny."[1]

It doesn't matter how the experience comes to you; you are in charge of your attitude toward it.

Even when your beloved moves through the life event we call "death," you have a choice in how to grieve. The Aramaic word for death, *meta*, means "not present here, but elsewhere." You can get angry with God or with your beloved—or you can give thanks for wonderful memories of the time you shared and pass on to others the gift that person was to you. It is only natural to experience anger, blame or sorrow in grieving a loved one. However, in time, you have the opportunity to choose a new attitude that will move you on to a new phase of living.

Each one of us is God in expression. The great thirteenth-century mystic Meister Eckhart said, "God did not become man in just one single individual. He has taken on human nature totally—therefore, He dwells in every person."[2]

You, dear friend, are God's beloved daughter or son—special, unique and important. You have every reason to walk 100 percent with an attitude of **delight**!

> **D**-ivine child of God that you are! Temple of the Holy Spirit!
>
> **E**-nthuse yourself with God, infill all you do with the Flame of Spirit!
>
> **L**-ove your life! Live your Love!
>
> **I**-llumine your path! Light up the darkness!
>
> **G**-ratitude is your attitude as you count your blessings!
>
> **H**-umble is your stance in the face of challenges!
>
> **T**-rue to your Self always! **DELIGHT** that ...

You were born to make manifest the glory of God that is within you.

[1] Neal Vahle, *Torch-Bearer to Light the Way* (Mill Valley, California: Open View Press, 1996), p. 75.

[2] Karl Otto Schmidt, *Meister Eckhart's Way to Cosmic Consciousness* (Lakemont, Georgia: CSA Press, 1976), p. 58.

The Secret in the Secret

WALTER STARCKE

"If, instead of praying for a thousand dollars,
we open ourselves to life's abundance
knowing our needs will be well met,
they will and with basketfuls left over."

The law of attraction can be applied in two realms:
the subjective or spiritual approach or the objective mental
one. Both approaches have value, but they are not the same.
However, we can have the best of both worlds when we
understand how the principle underlying the law of attraction applies at each level.

The difference between the mental/objective
approach and the subjective/spiritual one is simple. The
objective level is personal. It identifies a specific thing, condition or situation one wishes to attract and relies on one's
intelligence or value system to judge what is desirable and

what is not. In contrast, the subjective/spiritual approach is impersonal. Its goal is to activate spiritual principle and to be guided by higher consciousness with no specific or material results in mind.

Those who advocate the objective or mental approach believe that we should materially envision what we specifically want, draw a picture of what we wish to have, or specify the exact amount of money we believe we need. This objective approach has a particular preconceived object or goal in mind. What's more, it works! It is proved that we can mentally draw to us what we want.

However, such an objective approach is limited. It is based on trusting one's ability to mentally judge the difference between what is good for one to have and what may be evil. A person may want a sporty BMW convertible and can visualize it—see how it looks, imagine the details, and, sure enough, manifest one. That person may also drive down to the corner, get in a wreck, and kill himself or herself.

If the mental approach is accompanied with a strong sense of intuition, that can help assure a positive outcome when the mental approach is used. Nevertheless, the objective or spiritual approach is less fallible. When we turn the situation over to our higher consciousness, or whatever God is to us, we are assured that it will be for our ultimate good.

Today quantum mechanics adds scientific credence to the spiritual approach, as outlined in the beginning of the Gospel of John, which says, "In the beginning was the Word ... and the Word became flesh." Quantum physics proposes that consciousness is the substance of all that is, that consciousness creates everything in our lives rather than our having drawn things to us from outside. Thus we are not simply magnets attracting pre-made things to us, but rather *we ourselves create our lives and all that is in them.*

The quality of our lives is determined not by what we think superficially but by what we perceive as reality. Our perceptions manifest our reality. *The Secret* was on target in using the Winston Churchill quote, "You create your own universe as you go along."

As primarily thinking people, we do not know what is needed or in store for our growth and well-being. What we think we want to attract may be the thing that destroys us in the end. On the other hand, when we entertain and put energy into subjective (spiritual) ideas or ideals and do not outline them in specific terms (objectively), we initiate the same principle that is in the law of attraction; however, rather than drawing to us what we humanly think we desire, our divine inner selves create that which will be harmonious for us and in divine order. This is the secret in *The Secret*.

Here is an example: When we want companionship, rather than trying to attract a particular person who may or may not be what we expected, if we turn it over to Spirit and set in motion the consciousness of manifesting perfect companionship, when the time is right, that is what we will have. Similarly, if, instead of praying for a thousand dollars, we open ourselves to life's abundance knowing our needs will be well met, they will and with basketfuls left over. If, instead of trying to draw forth a specific automobile, we open our consciousness to the best and most appropriate transportation, that is what we will receive.

I promise you, when we trust the process and set subjective goals for ourselves, we will be shown how to create them or they will appear, without any down side. There won't be any crooked places to be made straight, and our rewards will be the result of our trust in the process and our perception.

The objective/mental and subjective/spiritual approaches are both valid and necessary at various times. It is not a matter of either/or. When we are sure that our inner guidance outlines a specific desired result, it can be expedient to apply the law of attraction mentally by outlining our goals. However, setting wise priorities is the secret to lasting success.

When we were given the two commandments to love God and to love our neighbor as ourselves, which is to say to love the subjective (cause) and the objective (result), we were also given an all-important and often overlooked priority: "Take no (anxious) thought saying, What shall we eat? or, What shall we drink? Or, wherewithal shall we be clothed? For your heavenly Father (your higher consciousness) knoweth that ye have need of all these things. *But seek ye first the kingdom of God, and his righteousness; and all these things shall be added unto you.*"

All for my highest & best good & grace a lease.

Trust the Chaos

Rev. Felicia Searcy

*"The Universe is responding to our wishes
and dreams by cleaning out the old worn-out images
we have of ourselves, along with the circumstances
that stand in our way."*

I watch people as they see *The Secret* for the first time. They get excited about the possibilities that are in store for them and begin to visualize the kind of life they desire while making plans accordingly. Folks start to take the necessary action believing that they are guided by a higher wisdom that is leading them to their dreams. Things start to happen and they feel good.

Then all of a sudden, the unexpected and uninvited begins to take place. That dream job someone just landed may not be what he or she expected. Many people may find themselves facing health challenges, unexpected financial obligations or strained relationships. They begin to wonder what went wrong and start questioning whether or not the law of attraction really works. They become skeptical and start to revert to old ways of thinking and acting.

This is when I encourage people not to abandon the new concepts just yet. I invite them to trust the chaos that is happening in their lives. In fact, the shifts that are occurring because of the changes they have made in the way they see things are the evidence that the principles *are* working.

Science tells us that two things cannot occupy the same space at the same time. *The Secret* tells us that thoughts are things. So in order to attract the things that we want to us, we must change our thoughts. As we change our thinking, our circumstances begin to change to match our new thoughts.

We understand this on an abstract level. The challenge begins when the changes unfold in the physical realm. As we change our beliefs, the universe begins to respond accordingly by eliminating those things that no longer match our new vibration of thinking. Spirit invites us to let go of old beliefs, circumstances and, often, people in order to make space for the new.

Up until this point, our belief system did not allow us to accept God's expanded version of our lives. We find that we settled for almost good enough. Once we discover that Spirit wants more for us, we can no longer settle for anything less than God's perfect vision for our lives.

It is scary to let go of what is familiar to us. Conditions may not have been the best, but at least we knew what to expect. Don't let what is comfortable hold you back. Trust the chaos and stay with the process so you can open yourself wider to receive more of God's good.

A woman in my congregation wanted a new, more fulfilling job closer to home. She became increasingly unhappy in her current situation and was desperate for something different. She called me one day to tell me that she had been offered what seemed like the dream job. The hitch was that it was farther from her home instead of closer. She had reservations but was sure that this new job was divinely delivered.

She began working and felt fairly satisfied with the work when one day about a month after she started, she went into work only to find herself fired. She called me that day shaken, questioning how this could have happened. She was sure that she followed guidance when she accepted the new job. She began to question herself, her process and her faith. Yet she was committed to working the spiritual principles she had learned in church. We were in fact starting a prosperity class that evening, so I encouraged her to come to class instead of isolating herself, especially given her new circumstances.

During the class sessions, she dug deep into her belief system. She did lots of forgiveness work and began to give thanks in all things. As a result, she saw that she had core beliefs that told her she didn't deserve good things and that she expected too much. Because of that, she saw how she had settled for something that wasn't quite what she wanted, afraid it was all she was going to get. By the end of the seven weeks she was able to see how Divine Order with her cooperation orchestrated the short-term job situation to give her an opportunity to heal some deep belief patterns that kept her from accepting her greater good.

Two months later I received another phone call from her. She had completed an interview earlier that morning for a job that was 15 minutes from her home. It was with a company that she believed aligned with her values, doing work that would allow her to expand her knowledge and skills. The employer initially told her it would take a week to make a decision. Instead, they called that afternoon to offer her the job. Not only did they give her the job, they said that they were not comfortable paying her what they had originally agreed upon. Because of her experience and qualifications they wanted to increase her salary by an additional $4,000 to a level that is much higher than the average in our area.

She realized that the chaos she experienced over the past few months was necessary to prepare her for this new opportunity. She saw that her old belief system didn't allow her to have the dream job she desired. She needed to do some deep healing so she could accept this gift into her life.

I am reminded of the times I have cleaned out a closet. I usually pull everything into the middle of the room so I can go through it. All of my stuff is spread all over the place in a huge mess. But, as I continue to go through things, discarding the old and keeping what is still useful, it all falls into place. When I am done, I see that I created order from the chaos. I see and appreciate what I have, with more room for new and improved things.

As we begin to work with the law of attraction to attract the things we desire, our world begins to shift. That is the time to relax and trust the chaos. The Universe is responding to our wishes and dreams by cleaning out the old worn-out images we have of ourselves, along with the

circumstances that stand in our way. We have all said yes
to the powerful presence of Spirit and have made ourselves
available to God's cleansing power. Let's trust this. Let's trust
the ensuing chaos and prepare ourselves for the wonderful
life that Spirit has created for each of us.

New Thought Is More Than What You Think

DAVID FRIEDMAN

*"The secret of why so many of us have trouble
applying the principles of* The Secret
*is that when we take on a new thought,
that thought often brings up feelings we're afraid of."*

"Our thoughts create our reality. What we think appears before us in the world. Change your thoughts and you change your life."

We know this. Why don't we do it?

With the recent popularity of *The Secret* and many other New Thought books and seminars, people are, more than ever, thinking that all they have to do is think a thought and whatever they want will appear.

In my experience, this is actually true. A new thought does create a new reality. But why then, when we take on a new

71

thought, do we often become discouraged and fail to follow through? We're not stupid. We're not lazy. We're not just missing the point. There must be something else to it, something we're not taking into account. There must be something that frightens us, some perceived danger that kicks in when we take on a new thought, causing us to drop the new thought and go back to the old one.

"The Thought Exchange" is a method I developed in which we look at our lives as though what we see before us is an *exact* mirror of our thoughts. When we see something in our lives that we wish to change, we ask ourselves the question, If this is an *exact* reflection of what I am thinking, what must I be thinking for this to be showing up? By answering this question, we often become aware of thoughts we didn't know we were thinking, thoughts like "I can't succeed," "I don't get to have anything," "I'm stupid."

Next we ask ourselves, Given what I want to see in the world, what thought might I think that would reflect as that which I wish to see? When we figure out what that thought might be, we exchange the old thought we were thinking for the new thought. Because the world is just a mirror of our thoughts, and a mirror *must* reflect what's in front of it (it has no choice in the matter), our new thought *must* appear in the world.

This often works well. But sometimes we find that when we take on a thought, it does not appear in the world. Because our thoughts always reflect in the world, and there's no such thing as a thought not "working," either we have not stayed with the thought or we have exchanged it for another thought.

Why would we exchange a thought that we *do* want to see reflected in our world for one that we *don't* want to see manifested? Some might say it's because we're sabotaging ourselves. But I say that we do it to protect ourselves. To protect ourselves against *feeling* something we don't want to feel.

The secret of why so many of us have trouble applying the principles of *The Secret* is that when we take on a new thought, that thought often brings up feelings we're afraid of. To avoid those feelings, we exchange the triggering thought for one that will keep us away from those feelings, even if it doesn't reflect what we wish to see in the world. Thus we keep ourselves safe from experiencing feelings we're afraid to feel.

It is a major misconception that when you take on a "positive" thought, you feel "positive." Nothing could be further from the truth. We can choose to think any thought, but we cannot choose the feelings that the thought brings up. Those feelings are often based on something that has happened in the past.

Let me give an example.

At a recent Unity retreat, each participant was asked to write a song and get up and sing it for the group. I was a group leader, and some of the people in my group panicked at the prospect of having to write a song and sing it. When I asked what they were afraid of, they said, "I'm going to be humiliated. People are going to laugh at me and ridicule me, and I'll die of embarrassment." As this was a Unity retreat, where everyone was there to be accepting and supportive, I pointed out that it was highly unlikely anyone would poke fun at anyone else, no matter what they did. Still, these individuals were frightened. When we looked into what they were actually frightened of, it became clear that they were frightened of feeling the way they had earlier in life when they had been in a similar situation and had been criticized or ridiculed. Because they didn't want to feel this again, even though they were now adults who could certainly tolerate whatever might happen, they took on the thought "I can't write and perform a song" to avoid being in a situation where that feeling might arise. To be able to write and perform the song, they would have to take on the thought "I *can* write and perform a song." Then they would have that feeling based on what happened earlier in their lives. If they could tolerate that feeling, they could hold the thought and go on to write and perform a song. If they could not tolerate the feeling, they would exchange the thought "I can write and perform a song" for "I can't do it," and thus avoid those feelings. Of course, they wouldn't get to write and perform a song either.

Here's another example. Let's say you want to run a marathon. The first thing you need in order to run that marathon is the thought, "I can run a marathon." Without that thought, you would never begin to run. But since you do think you can do it, you set out, holding that thought in mind. At mile 20, your legs are aching, your heart is pounding, and you're gasping for breath. If you decide that you can't tolerate those feelings, the easiest way to stop them is to exchange the thought "I can run a marathon" for "I can't run a marathon." Then you'll stop and you won't have those feelings anymore. You won't get to run the marathon, but you won't have to feel those feelings either.

Thus it is one thing to say that if you take on a thought you will see the result of that thought appear in the world, but that's only half the story. The real challenge is to help people hold onto a thought they wish to have, by assisting them in being able to tolerate and stay with the feelings that the thought brings up.

There are a variety of ways to work with feelings so you can maintain thoughts that will be reflected in the world as the results you desire. You can notice when you've exchanged the thought of what you want for a "protective" thought that keeps you feeling safe. You can understand that "negative" thoughts are not foolish or sabotaging, but rather like a drug we take to avoid the pain that arises when we take on a thought that scares us. When we stop taking the drug of thinking "negatively," we often feel pain. Inner child work can help; so can *affect tolerance* work, where the objective is not to abandon or change feelings that have upset us in the past but to learn how to feel them and be with them.

The problem we face in holding onto a new thought is not the traumas we have endured in the past, but the fact that there was nobody there to help us be with and feel the feelings those traumas generated. The real healing comes when we can simply feel those feelings. Being able to be with the feelings frees us to take on any thought, not just thoughts that will keep us from the pain.

Offering people the truth that thoughts appear as reality without offering them tools to handle the feelings that arise is like offering them a car without the keys. The principles in *The Secret* are excellent and true, but the secret behind *The Secret* is that, for many of us, those principles are unworkable until we understand and can tolerate and move through the feelings that come with them.

In truth, New Thought Is More Than What You Think.

Attraction or Perception: Which?

REV. PAUL HASSELBECK

"We determine through our beliefs and perceptions the people and things we attract ourselves to."

Much of the excitement around the law of attraction can seem more magical than metaphysical or even mystical. The law of attraction—like attracts like. We attract into our lives that which we think and feel about; that which we focus our attention upon is what is attracted to us.

But what about this? In the months prior to Y2K, as we neared the stroke of midnight, millions of people were thinking and holding beliefs about what would happen as the clock struck midnight. Many believed we would suffer a digital meltdown because the clocks in our computer systems were not designed to handle the turn of the century. People passionately held catastrophic thoughts and feelings and yet, when midnight came, doomsday did not arrive. Where was the law of attraction?

In pondering the anomalies of the law of attraction, I have come to two conclusions:

1) We do not so much attract things to us as we are attracted to those things, and

2) This happens through what I would call the *law of perception.*

Reporting on research by Dr. Rodolfo Llinas in her book *Quantum Leaps,* Charlotte Shelton said:

> While everything that we see, feel, taste, hear or smell is a potential candidate for perception, the information that actually enters our conscious awareness is only a small fraction of what gets filtered out. ... Our individual states of consciousness (e.g., assumptions, beliefs, thoughts and feelings) determine the choices that we make at each step of this perceptual process. Our perceptions are, in fact, shaped more by the information already in the brain than the external stimuli.[1]

I believe this is the primary way that the law of attraction works. As we focus on something we want, that something is not attracted to us like a magnet. Rather, our focusing on something alters the way we sort the incoming sensory data. We start perceiving our world differently. We actually begin to "search out" the something we want in our surrounding field of perception.

Here's an example. You decide you want to buy a Volkswagen Beetle. You begin thinking and feeling about owning this car. You visualize yourself driving this car to work, on vacations or on simple errands. This is the car you know and feel you want. And suddenly, you begin to see Volkswagen Beetles everywhere. But God or the universe did not magically put more Volkswagen Beetles on the road for you to see. <u>What has happened is that</u> you have begun to <u>perceive the world differently.</u> <u>You are sorting the incoming data differently through the power of your perception.</u> The Beetles had been there all along, in the background of your perceptual field. Now, seemingly by magic, they are every-where for you to see! It is not that they have been attracted to you; rather, you have *attracted yourself* to them.

This law of attraction via perception happens whether we do or don't want a new thing, situation or person in our lives. The person who keeps "attracting" an alcoholic into her life is not really attracting alcoholics. She simply has the uncanny ability to unconsciously scan a room full of can-didates and sort that incoming data through the power of her perception. She is holding powerful thoughts and feel-ings about alcoholics. She attracts herself to the alcoholic by sorting the incoming data. She can unconsciously read the nonverbal clues that scream "I'm an alcoholic." Similarly, the alcoholic in that room is sorting the incoming data. However, his perception can unconsciously read the nonverbal clues that scream "I'm codependent" based on past experience. So the two are attracted to one another like moths to a light. The light does not magically attract the moth. The moth picks out the light in its perceptual field and draws itself toward it. The light is simply being the light.

The law of attraction is a powerful law—not because things and situations are magically drawn to us, not because there is a power in the universe arranging things for us. It is powerful because it can remind us where the power has always been: right where we are. We attract ourselves to people, situations and things through the beliefs, attitudes and thoughts we hold, both conscious and subconscious.

We are all manifestors, applying the law of mind action from moment to moment. In fact, we cannot *not* work with the law. It is always operating, just like the laws of gravity and electricity are always operating.

The law of attraction via perception is not a passive law—we play the key, central, active role in our lives. We determine through our beliefs and perceptions the people and things we *attract ourselves to*. This is an enormous responsibility and an enormous opportunity. We can and must use the law to be the best Christ-selves we can imagine ourselves to be.

---

[1] Charlotte Shelton, *Quantum Leaps: 7 Skills for Workplace ReCreation* (Boston: Butterworth-Heinemann, 1999), p. 17.

The Bigger Secret

SCOTT KALECHSTEIN

"A heavy burden is lifted each time
we release the arrogant assumption
that we are so solidly in possession
of the big picture that we know what
our highest good is supposed to look like."

The Secret is out, way out. Those who have been entrenched in feelings of powerlessness are finding their mojo by applying its principles. Yay to the setting of intentions, the power of positive thinking, and the wondrous law of attraction! Yay to manifesting a perfect soul mate, the ideal income and our wildest dreams! Rock on, minds of mankind!

And while I am glad it has become so popular, I do have a few further thoughts to add to the conversation. When it comes to the law of attraction, I'm a bit of an outlaw. To me it's a little piece of the truth, and in the minds of egos wanting to play God, that can be a little danger-ous. I believe that letting people in on the creative power of thought without also giving equal emphasis to the law of *allowing* is a bit like teaching people inhaling without letting them in on an intimate and inseparable part of the process—exhaling!

To put it simply, the law of attraction is about how to get what you want. The law of *allowing* is about appre-ciating what you get; in other words, letting go and let-ting God, or seeking ye first the Kingdom. When applied together, these laws bring balance to the active and recep-tive male and female energies in each of us.

It's no secret that getting what you want doesn't automatically lead to lasting fulfillment. If that were the case, the bathroom cabinets of the married, rich and famous would not be filled with such an abundant supply of expensive antidepressant and antianxiety medication.

A Course in Miracles puts it bluntly: "The world I see holds nothing that I want."

Yet we all want what we want. But what's up with all this wanting? While wanting can be defined as desir-ing, it is also synonymous with lacking. "The Lord is my Shepherd, I shall not want" means that when we surren-der our attachment to a specific outcome and trust in the benevolence of the universe, we shall not lack. And that is the law of allowing.

When we get rigidly attached to a desired outcome, however, we are coming from the assumption that we are not whole beings until we get what we want. And that's an illusion that life delights in coaxing us to let go of.

Thaddeus Golas, in *The Lazy Man's Guide to Enlightenment*, said, "There is a good attitude to take towards any goal: It's nice if it happens, nice if it doesn't." Does that mean we are to be devoid of passion? No, just detached from craving an outcome, from thinking there is some tear in the fabric of God's perfection that needs to be stitched before we can fully enjoy being alive.

I love watching dogs run after seagulls on the beach. They set their sights on a flock and then are focused, single-minded and even passionate about running down a bird. At the same time, they are fulfilled in the thrill of the chase, having tremendous fun frolicking on the beach. Going home without having caught a bird doesn't for one moment diminish their love of life.

When we realize that just being alive is the gift that keeps on giving, we may pursue our own gulls just as passionately, but far less frantically. We value the process as much as the intended outcome. We embrace whatever we encounter along the trip with loving arms open wide, grateful for it all.

When we have tasted the nectar of a fulfillment that is not dependent on the outside world granting us our desires, we realize that life is blessing us as much when we don't get what we want as when we do. In those times we get to practice being friends with reality, letting go of our adversarial position to what is. A heavy burden is lifted each time we release the arrogant assumption that we are so solidly in possession of the big picture that we know what our highest good is supposed to look like. We get to more thoroughly chew on another spiritual slice of humble pie from *A Course in Miracles*: "I don't perceive my own best interests."

There's nothing wrong with having goals and using the law of attraction to manifest them. But you can attain the world, only to have your achievements magnify and intensify your inner turmoil. The ego's basic obsession with lack, that nagging sense of "not enough-ness," cannot be overcome by worldly success. When Jesus said his Kingdom is not of this world, he was speaking for all of us.

Even my mother, a devout, practicing atheist, will exclaim after the first bite of some fabulous dessert, "Out of this world!" (It has been said that there are no atheists in foxholes, and I would venture to add that there also aren't any biting into Junior's New York cheesecake!)

The Bigger Secret is that there is a state of being available to us that is not of this world. Echoes of it visit us ever so briefly; the first few morsels of cheesecake, the first few mouthfuls of romantic love and other fleeting moments of satisfaction. For some people who consistently choose to practice "Seek ye first the Kingdom," that state of being sets up shop and becomes part of their fabric. It becomes the foundation of a sense of self, rooted in eternity.

That's what I want—to abide in a love that is not of this world. Perhaps that's what we all want, even when we are seeking to manifest things of this world.

Have you had enough of a sense of not enough? Do you want out of the state of wanting that always leaves us wanting more? Let's remember together: "I am as God created me, and I am free, whole and complete as I am. I am enough, I have enough, and I do enough. I wake up from the dream of lack. I am drenched in abundance at all times. Every sunrise is proof of my infinite wealth, every breath is a miracle, and all is supremely and eternally well."

When that state of enough-ness takes root in you and permeates your being, you will most probably be moved to chase some gulls and have some fun.

Gangway ... I'll see you on the beach!

3.
Life Lessons

It Is No Secret

Stephanie Stokes Oliver

"Whenever I had doubt, I overcame it
by remembering what I had learned:
What He's done for others,
He'll do for you.*"*

I learned the secret—at least to my own life—when I was seven years old.

My mother was the director of my church's children's choir, and I was a member of the group of about 20 youngsters. That summer, a young church member and playmate of mine passed away suddenly at age 10. Singing at our friend Donald's funeral, we knew we would miss him, but we were taught that a funeral was yet another normal ritual of our church life, a part of God's plan. We all live, we all die—some folks in less time than others.

The main thing I recall about the funeral was the song we sang from the choir, overlooking Donald's little white casket:

"It Is No Secret." For many years afterward, I would sing it in
the junior choir. I even played it on the piano when I became
the choir's accompanist at age 14:

> *It is no secret what God can do*
> *What He's done for others, He'll do for you.*
> *With arms wide open, He'll pardon you.*
> *It is no secret what God can do.*

Listening to sermons was not my thing. It was too much
like being lectured to or being fussed at. But the music of my
church stuck with me like brown on rice.

I once heard comedian Dick Gregory say that babies
are more spiritual than adults because they had been in the
spirit world more recently. I don't know if that is true, but I do
feel that what we learn in those formative years stays with us.
What we internalize as children becomes part of our composi-
tion, character and lifelong knowledge. We learn to read and
write at an early age and that knowledge affects the rest of our
lives. So it is with our spiritual knowledge. I used to wonder
how my elders seemed so religious, so close to God, so willing
to worship with abandon. Now I know that although we may
feel inhibited to shout out "Praise God!" in adolescence, we still
may be sowing the seeds of faith.

When I turned 18, I left my loving family and church
home on the West Coast for college "back East," as the
church elders referred to it. It was an exciting time. I had
accomplished what my parents and community expected of
me. College was fun yet challenging. Through the exams and
difficult days, I prayed that surely I could excel because others had done it before me with God's help. Whenever I had

doubt, I overcame it by remembering what I had learned: *What God has done for others, God will do for you.* For me, that was no secret. It was just the truth.

I could see that life was good because of the wonderful things God had done for me and others. After graduation, I moved to New York City where life was exciting and dangerous. I found a church like the one I grew up in. The choir there also sang the song I knew so well. I felt at home.

After a few years of the career-girl single life emulating Mary Tyler Moore and *That Girl,* it occurred to me that it was taking more years than I desired to meet the divine-right mate. But hadn't I witnessed the fact that God had given good marriages to others my age and stage? Then why wouldn't I expect that to happen to me? Keeping the creed of "no secret" close to my heart helped me imagine myself in a strong marriage like that of my parents, with a love like the Temptations sang about, and the R-E-S-P-E-C-T Aretha commanded.

Whenever I read about a celebrity with a fine house and a finer husband, or when someone back home married one of the cute guys who wouldn't look my way, I'd work hard to suppress my envy by remembering that God's gifts to others were not exclusive. My blessing was on the way—maybe not now, maybe not when I wanted it, but in God's time. And God is always on time.

Indeed, I met my husband on 125th Street in Harlem one sunny Sunday afternoon. For a 24-year-old from Seattle, meeting Mr. Right was a big deal that didn't stay a secret for long. We were married in the same church back home where I had learned "It Is No Secret."

From childhood, I wanted to be an author. The books of
Laura Ingalls Wilder, Toni Morrison and Maya Angelou showed
me that women could write. Not having wealth to fall back on,
I knew I could not make a living as a writer—not in a way that
would give me a biweekly paycheck. Job security was important,
so I pursued a position as a magazine editor and was blessed
with a glamorous job at one of the top fashion publications.
Over the years, however, my deep desire to be an author did not
wane. I wrote at night when my husband and baby were asleep. I
took writing classes. I studied the success of best-selling authors.

My sister-in-law gave me the book *Creative Visualization*.
It helped me to see myself as an author. I envisioned myself
reading from my work at bookstores. Fingering the spines of
hardcovers, I would determine where my book would be shelved
in alphabetical order. Every chance I got, I attended the book
signings and publication launch parties of my literary friends
who were getting published. Suppressing jealousy with genuine
supportiveness, I would witness what was possible and affirm:
What God has done for others, God will do for you.

For years—20 to be exact—I endured rejection after
rejection from agents. It hurt me, but didn't stop me. It damp-
ened my spirit, but didn't deter me. I figured that as long as I
was going to be living anyway, I might as well be doing what
gave me joy. Writing was my creative outlet, so I pursued it in
spite of the setbacks. Eventually, after one agent who had taken
an interest in me moved away, someone in the publishing business who knew I was looking for a book deal told another agent
about me. Thank goodness, I hadn't let my embarrassment over
not getting published prevent me from sharing with everyone I
had met that I wanted to be an author. This acquaintance gave

the agent my number, and she called. It is now 10 years and three published books later. God's never failed me yet.

Jewel Diamond Taylor, a motivational speaker, says that "Fate is just another word for God." As Fate would have it, two of the books I have written have titles with the word *secret* in them. *Daily Cornbread: 365 Secrets for a Healthy Mind, Body, and Spirit* was inspired by Unity's *Daily Word*. The second book was called *Seven Soulful Secrets for Finding Your Purpose and Minding Your Mission.*

In researching *Seven Soulful Secrets,* I gained new knowledge of spiritual principles myself. The law of attraction is a universal truth that Myrtle and Charles Fillmore embraced in founding the Unity movement over 100 years ago. So that is no secret. Another fact that is common knowledge but not commonly embraced is that one can have all sorts of material things, but if a person is not in possession of purpose, life will not have meaning and sustainable joy.

In my book, I created an acronym for PURPOSE. Here's one for SECRET:

> S is for Sacred: Rhonda Byrne, the creator of the book and film *The Secret,* says "Use the sacred to create the secret."
>
> E stands for Eternal: A hymn teaches us, "As it was in the beginning, is now and ever shall be."
>
> C means Christ: See the Christ presence in all situations.
>
> R is for Religion: Use your beliefs to keep the faith in times of adversity.
>
> E equals Energy: Affirmative energy attracts like energy.
>
> T is the Truth: God is good and God is available; in fact, God is in you.

We package these concepts in the media as *secrets* or *codes* or *mysteries*, because people seem to want to feel that they are getting something they don't already know. Or making it a secret makes it seem special.

But the truth is that there is nothing that God withholds from you. God is good—all the time. As we say in Unity, it is God's great pleasure to give you the keys to the kingdom. There is no exclusive club you need to belong to. There is no buried treasure. It's all right here. It's out in the open. It's available for you and yours. There is no secret to the magnificent things God can do in your life.

Awaken to God's Grace

REV. CAROLYN THOMAS

"While perceptions, feelings, emotions, desires
and imagination shape our world,
we can be spared the full brunt
of negative thinking by God's grace."

It was a disorienting and painful time in my life. I had
recently divorced, changed jobs, moved to a different house,
and was just beginning to adjust to having joint custody
of my daughter. Each step toward establishing order in my
house helped me begin to orient myself to this new phase of
life. Yet night after night, I would slip back into disorientation, often waking up and not knowing where I was. When
this happened, I would first make certain where I was—in
this unfamiliar bedroom within a strange house that had not
yet become a home. Then, once I knew where I was, I would

awaken more fully and determine if my daughter Suzanne was with me or with her Dad. This nightly reorientation left me either thankful that she was with me or sad that she was not. With either feeling, my mind would spin as I struggled to get back to sleep.

I would think about how different life was from the dream I had held, different in ways I would have never imagined when I was newly married and embracing the American dream. My married life had held many good experiences at first, and I had no reason to think it wasn't a lifetime commitment. With the dream of starting a family came the anticipated joy and awe of creating one child and then another. Sometimes in the night, I would think about all the reasons why the marriage ended after 15 years. I would think about the hard times, two miscarriages, and about Suzanne's premature birth and the complications that nearly ended her life. I thought about loss. I thought about anger. I thought about blame. I thought about unrealized dreams. I thought about and grieved over the emotional pain each of us in our family of three had endured. Ending the marriage was my choice, and even though I knew in my heart it must end, I carried the painful emotions and the thoughts with me in every conscious moment.

One night I was awakened by a disturbing noise. I went through my mental check: Okay, I thought, I'm in my new house. Further awakening, I knew Suzanne was not with me. What was that sound that woke me? Could it be someone trying to break in?

Looking out from my second story bedroom window to my driveway below, I saw what had happened. Someone must have driven a car into my driveway to turn around and run over a neighbor's cat. Amidst the darkness and shadows, the nearby streetlight cast enough light for me to see the lifeless cat. Now my spirits plummeted. It was 2 a.m. I didn't know the neighbors and didn't know which one owned the cat. What could I do? I couldn't make myself face this situation in the middle of the night. I decided to wait until morning. After much tossing, turning and dread, I went back to sleep.

With the bright morning sunlight, I awoke, and for a moment was encouraged by the new day. Then I remembered the dead cat. I lay there for a long while, dreading what I had to face. Apprehensively, I got up and looked out the window. There in the driveway, in the bright sunshine lay a tree branch! It took a few moments for this scene to really sink in and for my mood to lighten.

In the darkness, my mind had translated this scene into one of tragedy. I had felt such pain, guilt, disorientation and darkness during the process of divorce that I had continued to color my world from a palette of dread and gloom. In the darkness of night, my thoughts and my imagination had teamed up to create a nonreality. I had been stuck in a pattern of expecting the worst. But on that morning I woke up to a new reality.

Some years later I read these words from James Dillet Freeman: "Imagination is the most entertaining and most frightening of all our faculties. It is the conjurer. It can beguile and bewitch us; it can frighten or enlighten us; it can lift us to ecstasy or plunge us to despair." Imagination and a depressed state of mind had transformed a tree branch into a dead cat and triggered the associated emotional and visceral response. Mr. Freeman went on to say that "our imagination may just be playacting what our hopes hope is happening or what our fears fear is happening."

That night was a profound wake-up call for me. It was as if a stage play was performed outside my window, complete with sound effects, props and spotlighting to get my attention. In my new awareness, I realized that I could choose to see life differently and begin to change my thoughts. I could begin looking at life in a new light, to refocus my thinking, and to embrace new possibilities.

I had known for some time that, though thoughts held in mind produce in the outer after their kind, what I needed to remember was that the negative thoughts I was clinging to and holding in my mind were also creating after their kind. The law works whether the thoughts are positive or negative. I can choose whether to create more darkness or more light.

I also needed to acknowledge another spiritual truth: that the grace of God can override and deflect the results of negative thought. While perceptions, feelings, emotions, desires and imagination shape our world, we can be spared the full brunt of negative thinking by God's grace. The light of a new day, the light of understanding, the light of God can transform the darkness and awaken us from fear to faith in a new and glorious dawn.

James Dillet Freeman's poem "Prayer for Protection" is a constant reminder of the Truth and can calm us and redirect our thoughts in the midst of any "dead cat in the night" experience:

The light of God surrounds me;
The love of God enfolds me;
The power of God protects me;
The presence of God watches over me.
Wherever I am, God is!

Operation Faith

REV. RALPH GRZECKI

*"My faith above all allowed me to let go
and allow God to guide the surgeon and
guide me to total healing."*

Have you ever experienced a life-threatening situation and come through it without knowing how you did it?

Such experiences are a testament to faith, and it is not blind faith. It is the result of understanding, embracing and practicing faith. An understanding faith is a faith that unconditionally accepts and knows that God is good and that all things work together for good. An understanding faith is a faith that works, even when one is not consciously aware of it. For many years of my life, I had been practicing and understanding faith without realizing it.

At the age of 63, I experienced the manifestation of an understanding faith that I had unknowingly been practicing for 22 years. During those years, I was able to pay off a huge debt, overcome a vicious addiction, complete college and seminary, and serve as a minister in Melbourne, Australia; Warren, Michigan; and Milwaukee, Wisconsin. One of the thoughts I had taken into my consciousness was that if anything very serious or life-threatening ever happened to me, Spirit would guide me through it. I would be led through because I believed I would be—that was understanding faith. I lived according to the law of mind action, "Thoughts held in mind produce after their kind," and believed that all would work out for my highest good, even if it was not evident at the time.

I learned the law of mind action through Unity, and applied it while studying for the ministry at Unity Village. I saw myself as a Unity minister even though it sometimes seemed a daunting goal. I still owned two flower shops in Detroit, Michigan. I was going to seminary in the morning, college in the evening, and serving a student ministry in Olathe, Kansas. Appearances indicated there was no way I could do all of this and yet, with God's help, I did.

I also held in mind that I was healthy, and that, if I did manifest an illness, the great healing power of God would see me through. Then came the ultimate proof that a faith built on understanding works even when we are not consciously aware of it.

One afternoon in March 2003, I found myself lying helpless on the floor of my office at home. I was sweating profusely, and I couldn't even turn over and crawl to a phone. I prayed, oh, how I prayed: "God help me get to that phone!" Eventually I did get to the phone and called Rosemary, the

executive director at our church office. I asked her to con-
tact my wife Carolyn and tell her to get home right away, as
I was not feeling well. I also asked Rosemary not to frighten
Carolyn. Rosemary asked if she should call 911, and I said
"No," adding that I could wait for Carolyn to get home.

But Rosemary did not listen to me! She called 911
anyway, and in minutes the ambulance was at our condo-
minium. Rosemary saved my life by not listening to me, but
by instead listening to the guidance of God. Spiritual law was
working no matter what I did.

After an MRI and CAT scan, I looked up into the
bright eyes of my neurological surgeon who said, "Ralph, you
have a brain aneurysm." He told me there was a 95 percent
chance of success with surgery. He said, "NOW!"

Carolyn and our board president were both at the hospital. As I was being wheeled into surgery, we stopped and
prayed together. With a kiss to Carolyn, I was on my way.

Down the long corridor to the operating room, I
began talking to God, saying, "God, I turn my life and all of
this over to you. I know you are here and in charge of all of
this. Should this be the last time I turn my life over to you,
I want to thank you for a great life. It was a fantastic ride!"
Next there was a smiling face telling me, "We are going to
put you to sleep now."

My aneurysm was treated through *clipping,* one of
the most common, effective and well-researched surgical
procedures for brain aneurysms. I woke up the next day in
ICU with 48 stitches in my head, the result of a successful
brain operation. I remained in ICU for another day, as well
as six more days in the hospital. It was not until two weeks

later that I found out what the surgery entailed. An incision had been made from above my eyebrows, around the skull and down in front of my ear. Next, a section of bone, or bone plate, had been removed from my skull. I later learned I had been unable to move and get to a phone because the artery in my brain had leaked.

I can honestly say that when I was told a drill and saw were used for my operation, I felt fear for the first time. Before that, I had not been told what the procedure would be. I did not need to know. Understanding faith was at work letting me know I did not have to know the procedure. In all honesty, if they had told me the details before the operation, I might have voted against it.

I had called on God twice: once when I wanted to reach the phone, and once as I went to the operating room, and that was to let it all go to God. Everything happened so quickly. Even the recovery was quick, and I am grateful for that also.

I took a battery of neurological tests, and the results were all in the 95 to 98 success percentiles. I lost no memory, eyesight or hearing. My physical tests went so well that I was back on the courts playing racquetball in 12 weeks and still play to this day.

Six months after my operation I was able to support and pray with a young man of 30 who was going through his own brain operation at the same Milwaukee hospital. He is a diver, and as we visualized his completely successful operation and healing, I told him I saw him diving again. He was diving within a year.

I have come to know that the faith I have in God works even when I may not know it is working. I believe the faith I have kept me from hearing what the surgeon was going to do. My faith allowed me to be serene and say yes. My faith allowed Rosemary to listen to God for guidance. My faith above all allowed me to let go and allow God to guide the surgeon and guide me to total healing. So much so that the scar above my eye is barely visible. What I believed, what I saw for myself, whether consciously or unconsciously, became my reality.

If it works for me in this manner, it can work for you the very same way. An understanding faith is a principle that works for all of us in any situation, even if we are not aware of it. The spiritual law works, no matter what.

The Secret of Weight Loss

BARBARA HADLEY

*"As long as I'm feeling loved and special,
I will just naturally make the right choices
about my food and exercise."*

My Journal, Day 1

I've learned this new idea: It's called the *law of attraction* and everyone has been talking about it like it's a big secret. I'm glad I finally got in on it!

I think this is the tool I've been looking for to finally lose the extra 30 pounds I've been carrying around. All I have to do is ask the Universe to support me in losing weight, make a poster that shows all these pictures of people who are thin and healthy, and imagine myself being the same way. Then I prepare myself to receive my weight loss.

There's no eating program or exercise; just by doing the treasure map and the asking and receiving, somehow my appetite goes down and I have a stronger desire to exercise. How cool is that?!

My Journal, Day 2

I've been practicing the law of attraction. I am a mighty magnet attracting my perfect weight! But it doesn't seem to be working, and I don't know why. I've made a treasure map of good-looking people, and I have imagined myself happy in a new bathing suit this summer. But the bulge isn't budging.

My Journal, Day 10

Yesterday I found out that I wasn't assuming the correct feelings. I misunderstood what the instructions "assume the very thoughts and feelings you will have when your heart's desire is made manifest" are supposed to mean.

I thought that to lose weight I should assume the feelings of happiness that I would have when I had achieved my goal. I've been telling myself, Isn't it cool that I did this? I've tried for a long time and I finally did it! Yea, me! But I wasn't losing weight. Now I can see that I was doing it wrong.

What I'm supposed to do is assume the thoughts and feelings I will have about the thing or experience I want— not the fact that I achieved it.

So it's more correct to think about how well my clothes fit and how vibrant my skin looks. Now I'm assuming these thoughts:

I am so happy my clothes fit, and they don't hurt! I am filled with joy because when I look in the mirror I see radiance. I am relieved of feeling overfed and stuffed, and I feel so good! I am filled with gratitude for all the good in my life!

These are the thoughts and feelings that are going to resonate with a healthy weight and attract radiance into my life easily and effortlessly.

My Journal, Day 14

Things are working better, but still not how I want. I haven't lost a single pound. But that's probably because I haven't mastered the skill of receiving yet. I realized yesterday that if I look really good at the pool this summer in that new bathing suit, I'm going to have to deal with the guys. Not sure I'm ready for that. Hmmm ...

My Journal, Day 20

Well, this is getting really frustrating. I'm all caught up in thoughts about weight and my body and clothes and guys, and I'm really overwhelmed with the whole thing. And I still haven't lost a pound. Thank goodness I haven't gained any!

My Journal, Day 24

Today is a new day, and I have discovered a new secret. I've learned some ideas from a place called Unity that I think might help. They fit really well with practicing the law of attraction. The difference is that in addition to thinking about how I want to look and feel, I appreciate how wonderful I am. I am a child of God. And through something called divine order, everything works really smoothly.

As long as I'm thinking and meditating about the special things God means in my life—the joy, happiness, abundance and love—and as long as I'm feeling loved and special, I will just naturally make the right choices about my food and exercise.

There's nothing supernatural about it—it is the scientific way things work. It's as scientific as gravity and electricity.

Here's what I'm doing. I trust that God loves me and would never tempt me with any food that is not good for me. So I just listen for that "still small voice" inside my head, and I know that God, the all-intelligent power in the universe, is leading me to make wise and healthy choices. I turn the decisions over to this higher power, and I know without a doubt that I am whole and radiant. Sometimes I hear other voices in my head telling me what I should do, but the still small voice is the one that makes my heart fill up, so I know it's the right one to listen to.

I want to continue affirming that my clothes fit and that I am filled with joy. I can see that these new affirmations make the law of attraction even more powerful because I have the strength, love and joy of God working with me.

My Journal, Day 31

I met the coolest guy today! He was walking out of the bookstore when I was going in and I bumped into him and we started talking and we sat and talked for hours! He knows a lot about the things I've been learning and I felt so comfortable talking with him. He even asked me out for tomorrow night.

You know, before I started thinking this way, I would never have had the courage to speak to him like I did today. It's really cool—I'm doing more than losing weight, I'm manifesting all sorts of good things in my life. God is really working through me to bring my highest good. I would have been happy losing some weight. But now I've lost five pounds, and I've got a date! Wow!

True Prosperity: Living Life From the Inside Out

SUSAN L. HOWARD

*"To truly understand the law of attraction
and how to make it work in our daily lives,
we must focus more on being than on getting."*

Unity co-founder Myrtle Fillmore said, "Sometimes we begin at the wrong end of the prosperity line."[1] If we are to attract all the things we want into our lives, then we need to build a true prosperity consciousness. "Seek ye the Kingdom of God and His righteousness" (Mt. 6:33 NRSV) and the promise is that all these other things that we want will be given to us as well. The only way to build a true prosperity consciousness is to start from the inside with a solid spiritual foundation. Everything else will follow.

If we are only focused on the outer, material things and the channels through which those things come to us and fail to recognize God as the source of our prosperity, then we are "at the wrong end of the prosperity line." When we understand that God is the source of all our good and that anything else that appears to give us our good is merely a channel through which Divine good flows, then we understand the practice of the Presence of God or the Kingdom of God in our lives. We are living life from the inside out rather than the outside in.

Intellectual understanding is a very important first step in the development of our consciousness. But understanding at this level also brings with it a temptation to use our knowledge for selfish or ego-centered purposes. Spiritual understanding is the quickening of the Spirit within that provides a deeper understanding, allowing us to be guided by wisdom. Spiritual understanding focuses on God as our source.

According to Unity co-founder Charles Fillmore, the law of attraction is "the law that all conditions in circumstances and affairs are attracted to us in accord with the thoughts we hold steadily in consciousness."[2]

It is not enough to have an intellectual understanding of the law of attraction if we are to build a true prosperity consciousness. To truly understand the law of attraction and how to make it work in our daily lives, we must focus more on being than on getting. The key is in practicing the presence of God.

David Owen Ritz developed a powerful class entitled "Keys to the Kingdom." Ritz states that if we are to experience true abundance, then it must touch every area of our lives: health, finances, relationships, career/creative self-expression and spiritual and personal growth. If we first seek to embody God qualities (such as peace, love, joy, wisdom) in our minds and hearts, then these God qualities will naturally begin to manifest in our daily lives as abundance in each of these areas.[3]

When we're living life from the outside in, we depend on external or material things to satisfy us, thinking that will make us happy.

When we live from the inside out, we focus first on being the spiritual presence we want to be. This empowers us to do what is ours to do, which brings us material and non-material wealth.

When our initial focus is on the outer, material things, we are only addressing the surface aspect of our lives. To open ourselves to greater abundance, we must go deeper—changing any thoughts, beliefs, ideas or attitudes that may be blocking our good. Nothing changes until our subconscious changes.

Positive, loving thoughts are far more powerful than negative thoughts. By emphasizing our spiritual growth first, we bring new positive thoughts of Truth into our consciousness. These higher ideas flush out anything unlike themselves. The right end of the prosperity line, therefore, is our inner spiritual life.

The first time I took the "Keys to the Kingdom" class, I created a very elaborate visioning board. I thought my wish was a "command" and I could order anything I wanted from the "catalogue of the universe" (*The Secret*). One of the things I "ordered" was a 20 percent per annum return on any investment I made. At the time, I was looking to reinvest my retirement funds. I did my research and invited the guidance of Spirit in this matter. I invested in only those companies I felt were socially responsible (governed by very strict ethical standards regarding labor laws, the environment and social impact). I knew this was good stewardship of my money. I then had the opportunity to invest in another venture. The promise of return was excellent and with the first couple of deals I had an approximate 20 percent return. In the last deal I made, my intuition screamed at me not to invest any more. I ignored it, and I lost my money.

When I invested my retirement funds, I consciously stood in the flow, acknowledged God as my source, and listened to the guidance of Spirit within. In the second venture, I ignored my intuition, failed to acknowledge God as my source, and erroneously saw my investment partner as my source. True humility is when we recognize that the human mind without the inflow of Spirit does not have sufficient understanding to use the law of attraction wisely.

When we focus on the external and live life from the outside in, we mistakenly think that happiness comes from "out there" and that all we have to do is figure out how to attract it. We only discover lasting, soul-satisfying happiness when we realize God is our source, and that source is within us and not dependent on anything external. Living life from the inside out happens when we put ourselves in God's abundant flow and allow that flow to express out into the world, through us and as us.

Each of us chooses, either consciously or unconsciously, to frustrate the flow or to allow its free movement when we choose whether or not to practice the presence of God. The late Unity leader and minister Eric Butterworth said:

We need a clearer understanding of the role of thought in consciousness. Thought of itself does not create. It either places us consciously in the universal flow or it frustrates the flow. If we think sickness or lack, we do not manufacture these things. When the thought is out of synchronization with the flow of life, then, even as anything cut off from its source, we come to know want. In the same sense, if we think health or abundance, we do not create these things. There is no way that man can create health. It is a flow or "flowering" of divine life. When the mind is stayed on the God-thought of wholeness, we are synchronized with the flow of life. When we think abundance, we are synchronized with the flow of abundance. We do not create it nor do we start or stop the flow. We simply accept it, giving our "consent" to its natural flow. This is what the Presence of God really is—the life of God present in us as an inexorable flow.[4]

As we gain spiritual understanding and practice the presence of God in our daily life, we mature spiritually. It is through the right use of our spiritual powers that we build a spiritual foundation for true abundance. As we spiritually mature and gain mastery over the spiritual laws of the Universe, we discover that the Kingdom of God is truly within and that if we seek this Kingdom, everything else will be given to us also.

"Let us rejoice that our good is in the realm of Mind where it is instantly available and responsive to our thought, word and need ... It is ours to use all that the Father has."[5]

[1] Myrtle Fillmore (Frances W. Foulks, ed.), *Myrtle Fillmore's Healing Letters* (Unity Village, Missouri: Unity House, 1948), p. 50.

[2] Charles Fillmore, *The Revealing Word* (Unity Village, Missouri: Unity House, 1959), p. 118.

[3] David Owen Ritz, "Keys to the Kingdom," 1989. *www.davidowenritz.com*

[4] Eric Butterworth, *In The Flow of Life* (Unity Village, Missouri: Unity House, 1982), p. 23-24.

[5] *Myrtle Fillmore's Healing Letters*, p. 51.

What Are You Doing Here?

Rev. Bob Uhlar

*"When you are in alignment
with your Divine Purpose, doors will open."*

Do you remember what you wanted to be when you grew up?

A boy in Spain wants to be a professional soccer player. He is a talented goaltender. And as he enters his college years, he plays for the junior Real Madrid team.

Late one night, when he is 20 years old, a car accident leaves him paralyzed from the waist down. With his dreams crushed, he lies in a hospital bed.

A compassionate nurse brings him a radio and a guitar and sternly demands he stop brooding and spend his time trying to play the songs he hears on the radio. As the months go by, he learns how to play the guitar. He starts to write songs of his own. Many express the angst of his crushed dream.

With his new passion for music, and intense rehabilitation, he is walking again in two years. He decides to continue his college education in England.

One day, to earn a little cash, he visits a record company that is searching for songs for its singers. Listening to the demo tape, the record executive asks why he doesn't want to record the songs himself. "Because I'm not a singer," he replies.

The Columbia Records executive had a different opinion. But until the Spaniard won the Outstanding Singer award at the 1968 Benidorm Music Festival, Julio Iglesias still thought of himself as an unlucky soccer player.

By 1983, Julio Iglesias was listed in the *Guinness Book of World Records* as selling more records in more languages than any other musical artist in history. He sold records in Spanish, German, English, French, Italian, Portuguese, Tagalog and Japanese.

Julio thought he should be a soccer player. But God had another plan.

The Secret focuses on using the law of attraction to draw what we desire into our life. But it is just as important for us to be giving something back.

Each of us has gifts, passions and talents to express in the world. One of the reasons we are here is to add something of value. There must be an equal exchange of energy in the world. In other words, there is no such thing as a free lunch.

We don't need to be doing something that is noble, will bring us fame, or will be a high-profile achievement. But we need to identify our Divine Purpose and focus our energy in that direction.

Some people have the misperception that some jobs are more important than others. Honor the fact that we all have our part to play in the Universe.

One man might know how to clean windows better and faster than anyone else. One woman may be the most compassionate caretaker for the ill. Another man might make the best fried chicken anyone has ever tasted.

So how do you discover your Divine Purpose? Ask yourself the following questions.

What do I *really* love to do? What am I passionate about? What do I really look forward to doing? What consistently brings me joy and exhilaration? What energizes me? "I found myself so focused that I skipped a meal and wasn't even hungry!"

What would you do if you were guaranteed you could not fail?

What do you do better than anyone you know?

Like Julio Iglesias, we find that other people tell us we do something well, even if we didn't think so. Often we are too hard on ourselves. Maybe you are a recovering perfectionist, like me. I needed to let go of the restrictive thinking I had accumulated in my childhood.

Here is another caution: Sometimes we know what we love to do. We share our plans with others. But they try to talk us out of it.

Why would somebody try to talk us out of our Divine Purpose? There are three reasons.

1. It is not their Divine Purpose. Think about it. You share your plan with somebody else. She pictures herself doing it. She realizes she would not like doing it. But instead of saying, "That is something I would prefer not to do," she says, "That's crazy! Why would you want to do that? That's awful."

2. You've triggered uneasiness in someone. You share your plan with somebody. He pictures himself doing it. He realizes that he would like doing it, but he is too scared to attempt it. Instead of saying, "That scares me," he says, "That's crazy! Why would you want to do that? That's awful."

3. "In the world you have tribulation; but be of good cheer ..."(Jn. 16:33 RSV). These "angels" have been sent into the world to test our resolve. They say, "That's crazy! Why would you want to do that? That's awful." But what they are really asking is, Do you have the courage and the resolve to follow through on your Divine Purpose and serve the world?

When we are doing what we love to do, we can handle the obstacles, the setbacks and the "interesting personalities" that God places on the pathway of our life.

It is also true that our lives have many chapters. We may do one thing for 15 years; then we are inspired to change direction and do something else. Some call it "midlife career change."

The important thing is that we acknowledge when our intuition is telling us that it is time for a major change. I'm not talking about a whim. I'm talking about the consistent, nurturing inner voice that is pushing us to change direction. We *know* the right thing to do.

We may not need to change our career. But it is important for each of us to know and express our Divine Purpose.

Start by setting aside two hours of time on the weekend to do what you really love to do. Make this a priority.

Don't talk yourself out of it. The positive energy that you are expressing will multiply and spread to the rest of your life.

If you do need to change your career, it may be scary. Start by looking for ways to express your Divine Purpose in a part-time or volunteer environment.

Many people worry that they couldn't make any money doing what they love to do. They are concerned that doors won't open to them. When you are in alignment with your Divine Purpose, doors *will* open. And you will discover doors in places you never would have thought to look before.

God will guide your thoughts with all the things you need to express your Divine Purpose. And you will prosper.

"A man's mind plans his way, but the Lord directs his steps" (Prov. 16:9 RSV).

Grandma Knew

REV. SHARI FRANKLIN

*"There are some aspects of life that
will forever remain a mystery to us,
such as children being born with diseases
and disorders, the transition of our loved ones,
or the unexplored regions of our own psyches."*

Grandma Swanson was my first spiritual mentor.
She was the only Sunday school teacher for our modest
brown stone church in my hometown in northern Nebraska.
Throughout her 50-plus years of service there, she lovingly
shared her wisdom and insights with multiple generations of
families. In my opinion, she was the best. She captivated our
young minds with her vivid stories and inspiring portray-
als of various Bible characters. Her focus was often on Jesus
and the rich depth of His faith. She would remind us that
it is indeed "according to our faith" that we can be healed,
guided and lifted up throughout life's journey. Our faith in

God can be all encompassing, giving us strength to deal with anything from problems on the playground to the challenges in our adult lives. Grandma taught us that God is in charge of the universe and that we have been given the gift of free will. We are responsible for our choices—among them, taking time to pray, listen and cooperate with God.

She taught us that faith is of God. We can *believe* in anything, but *faith* is about God and of God. God is the divine Creator of all life. We can believe in ourselves and one another; we can believe in our dreams and possibilities. But we exercise our faith in God to bring these things into reality.

Grandma would point out that God knows what is best—for us and everyone and every form of life. Sometimes not getting what we think we want is actually the best thing possible. When it came to making up our Christmas "wish list," as children we believed it was in our best interest to get everything on it. I remember wanting to convince God it really was for the best. Interestingly enough, we never seemed to get every item on the list. I remember asking Grandma about this. She smiled and assured me God loves us and "God always knows best." If I didn't get everything I wanted, how could that be the best? She added, "God works in mysterious ways. Have faith in God's infinite love for you and trust God."

Her response was a bit of a mystery, but in my heart I knew she was right. Decades later I learned the intriguing concept of paradox. Paradox is when two seeming opposites are both true. For example, God is both immanent and transcendent. God is within every atom and molecule of our being, yet God is greater than the entire universe.

Both concepts stretch our imaginations, and both are true. Similarly, God sees the big picture of life, yet God also knows the details of our needs and desires and how we are all connected. Everything we think, say or do affects the whole of life—though it seems to involve only us. We don't see the myriad ways in which one choice or action ripples out to the far side of existence.

There is a distinct and divine order to life and in life. From our limited human view, this can sometimes be difficult to see. In junior high school, I belonged to the Future Teachers Association. We took a field trip one spring to an enormous facility dedicated to the "mentally retarded," as they were labeled at that time. It served numerous residents with severe conditions, ranging in age from babies to adults. We were given a daylong tour. Some of those we visited were happy and laughing, while others seemed sad or sat with vacant stares, as if transfixed or hypnotized. I wondered what life was like for them. But even more, I wondered what purpose was served by their condition. We heard the statistics about mentally retarded babies who were not expected to live and those who were stillborn. I prayed to understand. I began to see the souls of these individuals, and I honored the journey of each one. I was not there to judge. I was there to bear witness to their lives—to honor them, bless them, and give thanks to God for their gifts. It was a lesson in unconditional acceptance and love.

This lesson has come back to me many times since. In 1990 I was a single parent with two young children, taking classes at our church to prepare for applying to ministerial school. The week after Mother's Day, my mom was diagnosed with multiple brain tumors. It was her third bout of cancer, and it was her last.

When I inquired about her condition, the oncologist said she was a walking time bomb, that he didn't honestly know how she was still alive, let alone coherent. I asked him to please not tell her that or give her a time limit. He agreed. As I prayed and asked God why, the response I received was to ask more effective questions. So I asked in prayer, "To what purpose does this situation and the cancer serve?" God gave me an answer that was a true paradox. It was time for her healing, for her soul to graduate to the next level of eternity. The cancer was the vehicle for her transformation and healing—not physically, but emotionally and spiritually. Her legacy to me was the gift of her love and what had been her home. God showed me she was opening the door for me to go to school in the immediate future, instead of waiting another 8 to 10 years.

Life does not come with a magic wand. There is no drive-through window or shortcut to enlightenment. Yes, we can be transformed in the twinkling of an eye. However, most of us take it step by step.

We are blessed with the gift of spiritual tools to use along the way. Tools such as the law of attraction and the power of positive thinking can greatly help us as well as others. We are all in this journey together. Yet even as we are co-creators with God on our journey, we are also subject to a divine order that is beyond our understanding. There are some aspects of life that will forever remain a mystery to us, such as children being born with diseases and disorders, the transition of our loved ones, or the unexplored regions of our own psyches. Paradox is the language of Spirit. Grandma knew.

Grandma also said there's more to the school of life than recess. She used the teachings of Jesus as a handbook for living, for guidance on how to *be*—how to walk our path in such a way that we are blessed and we are a blessing. She knew about living the paradox—honoring our hearts' desire while trusting God for our highest good. We may not always get the tangible things we want right now, but we *have* life, and we *can* live it abundantly.

4.
Shifting Consciousness

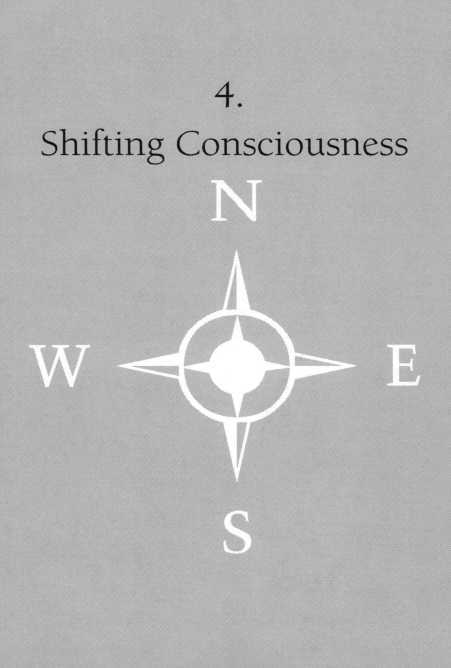

Consciousness
Is the Thing

Rev. Sylvia Sumter

*"Material things are temporal
and will fade away, but
consciousness is enduring!"*

The Bible tells us to think on whatever is true, noble, right, pure, lovely, admirable, excellent and praiseworthy. Whatever we hold in consciousness takes form in our lives. The physical world is the crystallization of consciousness. We can only change our lives by changing our consciousness.

Through affirmations and visualizations, we may manifest cars, jobs, mates and other temporary appearances, but what is the enduring wake of these manifestations? Have we added to consciousness what is true, noble, right, pure, lovely, admirable, excellent and praiseworthy, or have we added something else? And how long will it last?

Enduring manifestation requires a permanent change in consciousness.

Let's imagine that we are attempting to manifest a new car. Our goal is to get it and keep it without sacrificing anything else we are energetically financing, including our happiness and the happiness of others. How do we do it?

After prayer and meditation, it is time for affirmation and visualization; it is time to draw the car (the desire) nearer to us. However, during this process, we may find there are thoughts of fear, doubt and lack that rise up in our consciousness and inhibit the manifestation of our desire. So we continue to pray and meditate seeking clarity, healing and growth. We open ourselves to the answers and questions needed for clarity. Ultimately, Truth is revealed in consciousness and the blocks to our good are released. We have had a change in consciousness!

There is a saying, "Everything we have, we have by right of consciousness." The Bible states, "They that have, more will be given, and they that have not, even that which they have will be taken away." Thus, those who have the consciousness for what they desire will receive that and more; but those who do not have the consciousness for what they desire, even what they have will be taken away!

It is quite easy to manifest something; we do it all of the time because the laws of *manifestation* and *attraction* are always at work, even if we are unaware of them. The greater task is the ability to maintain whatever it is that you have manifested. For that, consciousness is a must! You must have the ability to not only draw a thing to you but to keep it as well.

Consciousness is the accumulation of thoughts, feelings, attitude, perceptions, beliefs and values held over time. Consciousness grows and expands as you gather energy and focus on your thoughts and feelings. It becomes part of who you are. It reveals your inner world and speaks to your deep-seated beliefs.

Suppose you were able to attract something you had wanted for quite some time; however, you were also afraid of not getting it or thought you might be unworthy of it. Or perhaps you weren't sure it was right for you. You would most likely not be able to keep or maintain your manifestation because you do not have the consciousness for it. You really don't own it in heart and mind; you simply manifested a temporary coup. As the Scripture states, "Even that which you have will be taken away!"

The Bible also says "Seek ye first the Kingdom of God, and all these things shall be added unto you." Material things are temporal and will fade away, but consciousness is enduring! When you build and establish a Kingdom-of-God consciousness, things will begin to come to you naturally and easily because you dwell and vibrate on a higher level or spiritual plane of consciousness. You are in touch with substance, the spiritual energy that lies in back of all things. And, from the invisible substance of God, you naturally draw forth whatever is needed or desired for your highest good, under grace. Consciousness is the thing!

While the law of attraction may be the best-kept secret, understanding consciousness will be the Truth that sets you free.

Living in the Love Vibration

SHIRLEY MARSHALL, PH.D.

*In this state of being, we are heart-centered
in thought, word and deed.
We project the high frequency of
love and light, and it returns to us."*

Well into midlife, I've finally discovered that the law
of attraction means living in the love vibration. Not only
is this the law of attraction, it is the law of life. If we want
good to manifest for us, we must commit ourselves to feeling good, being good, doing good. Good is God expressing
through us.

When we live in the love vibration, our energy reso-
nates at a high frequency and we express the God-qualities
of compassion, forgiveness, tolerance, respect, generosity, joy,

peace—all that inspires, empowers and enhances life. The love vibration lifts us to a higher state of consciousness and frees us of the thoughts, feelings and actions that minimize and victimize us. Gone are any neurotic fear, guilt, judgment, greed, envy, arrogance and the ego's stubborn need to be right. "Vexations of the spirit" lose their power over us. Free from the baggage of negativity and limited thinking, we begin to feel lighter and shine brighter. We become the magnet attracting our good.

"Living in the love vibration" may be a simple concept to understand, but it can be our most difficult challenge. Living in the love vibration means keeping our ego/personality in check as we relate to people and circumstances from "the high watch," our soul-self. Our ego easily indulges in the dramas of life. We invest emotional and physical energy in advancing the ego through superiority, security and status. Our soul-self is the wise, detached participant-observer. It experiences life but is not consumed by it. It recognizes life as the unfolding of a Divine Plan, the evolving of Spirit within form. The soul-self trusts that "all things work together for good."

When we live in the love vibration, we *know* that all aspects of life are connected and that we each have the potential—indeed, the responsibility—to become whole. To clarify: Connection means that every presence on this planet (human, animal, plant, mineral) is a unique expression of God and that we are all interdependent. There is no separation ... we are all cells of the living God, and what affects one, affects us all. Wholeness, on the other hand, means being complete as an individual and in harmony and balance at all levels of our being—body, mind and spirit. To be whole means to gather up and heal our fragmented pieces—the parts of ourselves that are disconnected from Spirit. Our brokenness is often due to feelings of unworthiness and pain from the past. Living in the love vibration keeps us focused in the present moment, connected and at one with ourselves and all there is.

Some people are born with a high love vibration, and others are fortunate to grow up in it. Most of us, however, have considerable overcoming to do in order to fully experience it. This overcoming is the process of personal transformation or the process of becoming connected and whole.

Living in the love vibration is our birthright and directs the unfolding of our life's passion. It sets the intention for every day, the agenda for every interaction, the prescription for every ill and the expectation for every circumstance.

In this state of being, we are heart-centered in thought, word and deed. We project the high frequency of love and light, and it returns to us. This is the law of attraction. Because the love vibration requires our ego personality to surrender to the soul-self, we get out of our own way. Our path is cleared. We encounter people and situations that inspire us and guide us toward the fulfillment of our potential and passion. We are in the flow of life. Our role shifts from reactor to co-creator. We are empowered.

You know when you're living in the love vibration because you can feel it. It feels like a natural high. It is a feeling of connection, of wholeness, of lightness and expansion. Meditation, miracles of nature, emotional ecstasy and places of awesome beauty can give us similar feelings of bliss.

To continually live in the love vibration takes considerable commitment and vigilance. It is all too easy to regress into fear, judgment or self-righteousness. No matter how spiritual we think we are, we are still having the human experience of trials and tribulations, progress and relapse. And it's all right. We don't have to deny or condemn our human vulnerabilities. The goal is to be positive and let the intelligence of our heart guide us. Similar to the practice of Alcoholics Anonymous, we just need to take it one day at a time. It can be helpful to set our intention each morning during meditation, prayer or in the shower—whatever works for us. Being mindful of the intent, we chart the day's course and can more easily self-correct when we stray.

Prayer, meditation, inspirational readings and service to others are all excellent ways to attract connection, wholeness and love. Other strategies include:

- Seeking the good in everyone and everything.
- Bringing trust to adversity.
- Being grateful for all that we have.
- Taking the high road in any conflicted situation or relationship.
- Creating a sacred space of peace and beauty in which to renew.
- Caring for living things.

If the law of attraction is about living in the love vibration, can it also be about growing wealth and materialism? Certainly, if this is what our potential and passion manifest. There are no limits or conditions placed on God's good. It's not about what we have or don't have in the physical, material realm; it's about how we live. We can live the love vibration as a prince or a pauper, a CEO or a cashier. Wealth, however, can easily tempt and trap, thus requiring even greater commitment and vigilance to stay on course.

Love is the elixir for joy and the antidote to pain. Love fuels the fire of our passion. Love lifts us from our limitations to our potential. Love transcends time and space. Love transmutes differences and prejudices. Love heals. Love is the vibration of Spirit, the song of the Universe. Love is the Alpha and the Omega.

Learning to live in the love vibration is why we are here. It is our individual and collective purpose. It is the secret of life that is hiding in plain view. When we live in the love vibration, we graduate this life with honors.

Letting Versus Getting

Rev. Beverly Saunders Biddle

*"For this world to more fully reflect
the goodness and grace of God,
we must shift our consciousness away from
identification with outer manifestation."*

The law of attraction is misapplied when the focus is on manifesting things without the requisite spiritual foundation. When people who are not grounded in metaphysics or practical spirituality attempt to "use" the law rather than aligning themselves with it, they may fall prey to a consciousness of getting.

Some people have denigrated the law of attraction as hocus pocus or idolatry, or have said it absolutely "did not work," as if it were some magic potion or magic wand. In American culture, people are so focused on instant gratification that many are seeking a quick fix. They are not willing to make the commitment to building spiritual consciousness that ultimately does result in attracting all of God's abundance.

Those seeking instant results are looking outside themselves for the answers to internal questions. People who have not been successful in certain areas of their lives often look externally for the reason.

What is missing is a willingness to look within—to grow. We anchor our oneness with Spirit as we align ourselves with universal law and apply spiritual principles out of devotion to God. Spiritual tools have come to be seen as ways to manifest material goods rather than letting in the goodness that is our birthright.

As more people understand how God's law operates, and the principles behind it, the more attributes of God will unfold in our world: love, harmony, peace, wisdom, joy and prosperity. For this world to more fully reflect the goodness and grace of God, we must shift our consciousness away from identification with outer manifestation.

The key is *inner* manifestation, which then out-pictures into our world. As we build spiritual consciousness, this shift automatically occurs. We first unify with God, knowing there is no separation between us and God, nor between us and anyone else. This is a fundamental Truth. When we know this, we realize that all that the Father has is ours—that it is the Father's good pleasure to give us the kingdom. We see, then, that there is no-thing we lack. We know that all that God is, we are—all the attributes that are of God are the Truth of who we are. This reduces our seeking answers outside ourselves. Instead, we experience an inner knowing and an inner peace that passes all understanding.

Building spiritual consciousness requires that we not only study spiritual laws and principles, but also apply the truth we know. One of the fundamental teachings in Unity is "Knowing and understanding the laws of life, also called Truth, are not enough. A person must also live the truth that he or she knows." Our lives become a spiritual practice.

The late Unity leader and minister Eric Butterworth wrote that Truth students are too often over-read and under-done. He encouraged us to apply the truth we know in the way we live our lives. One of my personal mentors, Rev. Dr. Iyanla Vanzant, who was herself mentored by Rev. Butterworth, says that learning has not occurred until behavior changes. We must use the information we know in order to anchor it in our consciousness and make it meaningful in our daily lives.

We are being called to take our knowledge to the next level—even the next dimension. We must go beyond intellectual understanding of the laws and principles to experience what Charles Fillmore called a "quickening of the Spirit within."

As a minister and spiritual teacher, I continually emphasize to Truth students the importance of praxis. *Praxis* is a Greek word meaning "practice," as opposed to theory; i.e., the application or use of knowledge and skills. It means consistently practicing what we know to be true—not just on a daily basis, but hour by hour, moment by moment. Praxis requires vigilant and diligent awareness of where we are in consciousness at any given time. What are we thinking, feeling, believing? It's being conscious of fears or judgments that may be obscuring our blessings; the unwanted sentiments in our hearts and minds that may be blocking the manifestation of our highest good.

This vigilance requires that we understand all of the spiritual laws—not just the law of attraction—so we can live in alignment with them. The laws are always operating in perfect order. The laws of mind action, cause and effect, polarity, vibration and other universal laws guide us in living full and abundant lives.

In addition, we study spiritual principles so they become a part of the very fiber of our being. We have not only an intellectual understanding but also a spiritual understanding of them. We know faith, truth, love, peace, integrity, harmony, belief, commitment, and so on in a fuller, more integrated way. This deeper understanding guides us in our daily living.

We further deepen our spirituality through consistent prayer and meditation. These practices raise our vibration and provide an opening for Spirit to work in, through and as us. In addition, we can use intention, affirmations and denials to clear away the obstacles and set us on a clear path to greater good in every arena of our lives.

As we lift our consciousness and daily demonstrate spiritual laws and principles, our lives become reflections of God's glory and God's grace. We allow God to move in, through and as us, guiding us to our highest good. We dedicate our lives not to getting, but to letting.

Spiritual Alchemy

REV. KELLI JAREAUX

*"The law of attraction draws to us
that which we are in consciousness."*

The Hollywood movie *The Prestige* is named for the most amazing part of a magician's act, when the trick reaches its climax and an incredible outcome is revealed. It is amazing, yet, at its core, it is still a trick! If we were to see a magician change base metal into gold, we would know that somewhere, the magician had stashed the metal and that the gold existed long before the trick was performed. Not so with spiritual alchemy.

With spiritual alchemy, the Holy Spirit actually transmutes a thing into a completely new and different thing. Holy Spirit does not transmute metal into gold in the physical realm; it transmutes metal-consciousness into gold-consciousness. When we use the law of attraction to manifest, we can choose to do so from either a metal consciousness or a transmuted consciousness of gold!

Spiritual alchemy is grander than any trick. It creates an actual change in consciousness. With or without that change, the law of attraction draws to us that which we are in consciousness. A metal consciousness will draw metal; a gold consciousness, gold!

Affirming and visualizing are part of the alchemical process, but not the only part. Affirming and visualizing alone merely shift energy, causing a spike in our vibration. A spike is not a permanent elevation. If we expect to sustain what we have created, we must in consciousness become the substance of our desire and stay that way.

For example, if at our current vibration we are unable to energetically support a new relationship, through affirmations and visualizations we can refocus our energy. Like squeezing a water balloon, we can redirect and compress the contents of consciousness, causing a temporary elevation that manifests our desire. However, affirming and visualizing alone will not increase our baseline vibratory level. It would remain unchanged. The old thoughts, feelings, beliefs and behavior patterns that kept us in lack are not healed.

Spiritual alchemy permanently changes consciousness. It does not simply squeeze the balloon. It changes the balloon's contents. Instead of circumventing growth for fast and fleeting results, we can permanently use existing energy differently or add new energy to permanently raise our vibratory level.

Spiritual alchemy transmutes our fears and flaws. Unless our fears and flaws are transmuted, our manifested desires will be the embodiment of not only our desires, but also our error thinking. In this sense, our manifested desire may become a mocking reminder of subconscious feelings of unworthiness, ultimately causing our compressed consciousness to revert to its former state.

The law of attraction is best applied not through spiritual sleight-of-hand or manipulation of consciousness, but by doing the work to heal and grow. If, for example, our goal is to find and keep a new relationship, we must trust the process, not attempt to circumvent it.

The process begins within. It begins with prayer, meditation and catching the vision of how God expresses beauty through us. It requires surrendering to the internal yearning and the external learning. *Then* we affirm, deny and visualize. We squeeze the balloon of consciousness, not to shortcut the process of attracting our desires, but to reveal why we don't already have it, to reveal our fear, to reveal the aspects of consciousness that are in resistance, to see why we are pushing our desire away. In drawing our desire closer, we can learn about it and about ourselves. This learning is critical!

Next, as we continue to pray and meditate, we seek clarity, healing and growth. We pray to open ourselves to the answers and to the appropriate questions. Ultimately, the answers come. We come to know what we are afraid of, what we are running from, and why we are hiding from our good. And we begin to grow.

The fears and flaws in consciousness are the jewels of the alchemical process. Perhaps by ignoring these jewels, we could hasten manifestation, but our goal is beauty and alchemy, not speed. After all, we and all emanations of God are eternal!

In truth, fears and flaws don't disappear when we ignore them. They stay with us, muttering relentlessly until we hear them. They may be minimized on the screen of consciousness, but their program is still running. It is not closed, it has not been deleted from the system, and it is still attracting and drawing manifestations of itself. To delete the program, we must open it, explore it, run a diagnostic, discover why it has popped up on the screen and what it is trying to tell us. Fears and flaws also are God's gifts. Gratitude directs not that we open them, but that we allow them to open us, to grow us.

When we ignore fears and flaws and focus only on our desires, our consciousness enters a state of protection, protecting us from a part of ourselves. Stagnation is the result. Biologists tell us that nothing living can grow in protection mode. All growth occurs by moving toward the stimuli. Thus, we grow and trigger spiritual alchemy by moving toward our fears and flaws.

Fears and flaws are our textbooks. We cannot graduate without learning from them, and we cannot circumvent them. When (even as we are affirming and visioning) we treat fears and flaws as our growing edge and go into them, we lay a firm foundation for enduring manifestation. When we transmute a fear, we do a deeper work than mere energy shifting. We free energy once expended to fuel fear so that energy can be expended on something valuable. We permanently restructure consciousness. We grow and awaken new energy into our vibration. We permanently increase our vibration and restructure consciousness so that our energy is used to fuel aligned desires, rather than unaddressed fears.

In short, if maintaining our desires requires a certain vibration, our goal must be to actually vibrate at that level. While it is true that we can temporarily "jury-rig" consciousness to get what we want, if we manifest from this stagnated state, the very fears and flaws we seek to avoid will be inherent in our manifestation. More significantly, manipulating consciousness robs us of the opportunity that lies dormant in our fears, our flaws, our unforgiving, our resistance; the opportunity to move to the place Spirit is nudging us toward; the opportunity for healing and growth and the benefit of the beautiful, enduring manifestations that spring forth as the natural consequence of truly elevated consciousness.

The Middle Is Moving!

REV. WENDY CRAIG-PURCELL

*"We are, indeed, living in exciting and new times.
A new world is truly waiting to be born."*

The principles to create a new world—a world that works for everyone—have always been with us. But the consciousness has not always been there. The methodologies have not always been there. And the tools to connect people with the information they need and with others of like mind have never been there before in the way they are now. We are, indeed, living in exciting and new times. A new world is truly waiting to be born.

As we all know, and as *The Secret* author Rhonda Byrne admits, the law of attraction is not new. Universal principles never are or they would not be *universal principles*. The principles of aerodynamics did not suddenly come into existence when the Wright brothers had their first successful flight at Kitty Hawk in 1903, any more than the principles of gravity came into existence when the apple fell on Sir Isaac Newton's head and caused him to question why. What came into existence—or more accurately, into awareness—was the *understanding of* and ability to *consciously use* these laws. Similarly, while the law of attraction has been taught in New Thought for more than 100 years (and by others as far back as ancient Greece), what is new is how voraciously it is being consumed by the mainstream, the vast segment of society in the middle. "Race consciousness," as Unity co-founder Charles Fillmore might call it, is being influenced and changed. That is exciting, powerful and enormously important.

Why? Because when the "middle" of society shifts upward and becomes more consciously awake (that is, when race consciousness is elevated), the sheer impact of those numbers can help pull the rest of humanity upward and forward. Jesus said, "If I be lifted up, I will lift up all men unto me" (Jn. 12:32). This movement is critical if we are going to bring forth a world that works for everyone.

While humanity has unquestionably benefited from the spiritual awakening and teachings of the great sages and avatars such as Jesus, Buddha and Lao-Tzu, what is desperately needed today is the spiritual awakening (and the enlightened, compassionate living borne of such awakenings) of each and every one of us. Although there will always be instantaneous awakenings—those that happen in the twinkling of an eye, such as Eckhart Tolle's or Byron Katie's—for most of us, awakening moves through four fairly distinct stages.

The first stage is the "to me" stage. This stage is characterized by varying degrees of suffering and victimhood.

"Life—especially 'bad' things—just seems to happen to me." "Nothing ever works out for me." "I always seem to be in the wrong place at the wrong time." "Why can I never have or get what I want?" We ask "why" not so much for understanding, but so we can know who or what to blame for our circumstances. In this stage, we are asleep. Our minds are undisciplined. We have no awareness of the power of our thoughts to create. Our lives are being "created" unconsciously and by default.

The second stage is the "by me" stage. In this stage we start to wake up—often as a result of some painful trigger: a serious health challenge, a significant loss, a traumatic event. We ask "why" and we sincerely want to understand our relationship to the circumstances of our life. We begin to claim our power. We find our voice. We learn that we have the power to change our lives; that we are not victims or innocent bystanders to our lives, but are, in fact, conscious co-creators of our lives. This stage is characterized by greater self-awareness, accountability and drive.

The move from the first stage to this second stage is dramatic and life-changing. We are hungering and thirsting for a better life for ourselves. *The Secret* speaks to this hunger and thirst for better and more and shows us how to use the law of attraction to satisfy that hunger and thirst.

But true—or full—awakening does not end in a life focused on "self" and material acquisition. It matures and deepens, moving through a third and fourth stage—"through me" and "as me." Here our use of Principle is not only conscious and co-creative, but also very compassionate. Here we question not only what we desire, but why we desire it in the first place. Here we feel our oneness with all humanity and the responsibility that comes from knowing we are one. Here it is not enough that we are happy and that our lives are working; we want a world that works for everyone. Here we seek maturity, clarity and purity so that we may be used as a vehicle through which Spirit moves. Here we use the law of attraction not so much to manipulate the universe to get what we want, but to be used by the universe to bring about the world It wants.

We are in a time of great spiritual awakening and we are blessed to have so many different factors working together to help nurture this awakening. In the past we had only a few at the leading edge of spiritual development pushing forward. But today, the middle is moving forward, the mainstream is starting to awaken spiritually, and race consciousness is shifting. We are riding a cresting wave of good that is strong enough and powerful enough to transform our world with love.

5.
Other Sacred Secrets

Discovering the Law of Attention

PAULA GODWIN COPPEL

*"If we want deep peace,
abiding love and lasting happiness,
we need only wake up to the heaven
that is already here."*

Millions of people have become enamored of *The Secret* as a way to achieve more abundance in their lives. Newly empowered by the law of attraction, they are busily conjuring images of what they want—holding their desires in mind and asking the universe for the cars, jobs, money, partners, vacations, whatever they believe will make them happy.

There is no real harm in applying *The Secret* this way. However, it does perpetuate a disturbing underlying premise: the idea that something is missing and that we must find—or attract—that thing in order to be happy and whole. The very word *attraction* implies that we must bring something else into our lives in order to be complete.

Madison Avenue was built on this concept and indeed relies on it every year to sell billions of dollars worth of advertising. We often fall prey to these ads, buying everything from makeup to medicine in order to find happiness.

But deep down, we know better. There is something in us that knows, if only on the subconscious level, that we are already whole, perfect and complete just as we are. Our peace and joy come from within, not from outside. We are created in the image and likeness of God, and it is God's good pleasure to give us the kingdom, right here, right now. There is nothing to "attract" because nothing is missing.

Jesus said, "The kingdom of heaven is at hand." What else could we possibly want?

An honest answer would be: We want to know this heaven. We want to see it and experience it, every day.

And for that, we need a deeper secret than the law of attraction. We need what I would call the *law of attention*. For although it can be entertaining to manifest outer things, what we manifest on the outside is less important than what we manifest on the inside. If we want deep peace, abiding love and lasting happiness, we need only wake up to the heaven that is already here.

When we enact the law of attention—when we apply the power of our perception to a full experience of the present moment—we are lifted to a fuller awareness of our oneness with God and with all of creation.

Applying the law of attention doesn't take years of study. It doesn't require buying, attracting or pursuing anything. It happens simply through a shift in focus—and the reward is instantaneous.

A few years ago, I experienced the power of attention in a most moving and memorable way.

I had been reading Eckhart Tolle's landmark book, *The Power of Now*, noting how often I was not fully present in my daily life. In particular, I realized that I often half-listened when my children, Ben and Emily, were talking to me while I cooked and cleaned.

One night, I decided to respond differently. As I was setting the dinner table, Emily, then 13, came in and began telling me about a problem with a friend. Instead of continuing my task and answering her with rote "uh-huhs" and "really?'s," I put down the silverware and turned full around to face her. I looked right into her eyes and focused entirely on her and every word she was saying

After a few seconds, my attention on her became so intense that the room around us disappeared. I lost all sense of self and felt as though I was falling into her—into the pools of her eyes, into her soft voice and tender heart. I felt overcome by my oneness with her, and tears filled my eyes.

A few weeks later, I told a spiritual mentor about this experience with my daughter, trying to make sense of it.

"I felt like I was falling into her," I said.

"You were," said my teacher. "You were falling in love."

Yes, that was it. Once the distractions were cleared, once I was totally present, the way was open for a rush of love.

Interestingly, I have had similar experiences with perfect strangers in a Unity class or workshop when we were instructed to look into one another's eyes for a minute or two without speaking. While this exercise initially feels awkward and uncomfortable, invariably a deep connection occurs. I typically find myself moved to tears, having looked into the soul and humanity of someone who is both unknown to me and yet, through the great interconnected web of life, part of me.

Unity's poet laureate, James Dillet Freeman, captured this state of being in his beautiful book, *Be!*:

> I have walked down a street crowded with
> strangers when suddenly they were not strang-
> ers and I felt myself expand and take them in.
> I felt their loneliest longings, their loftiest aspi-
> rations, their hopes and fears, their love and
> faith and joy. I was the self that transcends self,
> the larger self that is not bound by space and
> time, the self that knows that it is one with the
> reality in all people.

It thrills and amazes me that this mystical oneness can be achieved with anyone or anything, at any time, by being fully attuned to what is before us. What we give our attention to grows before our very eyes. When we pay close attention, our perception takes us deeper and deeper still.

Poet William Blake expressed how wonder-filled this awareness can be when he wrote:

> To see a world in a grain of sand
> And heaven in a wild flower,
> Hold Infinity in the palm of your hand
> And Eternity in an hour.

Such insights remind us that the simple pleasures are the deepest. The most fulfilling moments in life are not characterized by complexity, or acquiring or possessing. They are a product of simple awareness, pure consciousness and love.

The law of attention opens the way for our connection to the divine. We sharpen our focus on what is in front of us, and feel ourselves become open and receptive. At such times, we see with soft eyes. We perceive the highest and best in others. We are attuned to the voice of God.

Some of my most inspiring teachers in this practice have been animals, who surely provide the greatest examples of living in the present moment. While they do not have the intellectual abilities of humans to reason, plan, imagine and so on, neither are they encumbered by the complexities we self-create. They live in pure simplicity, for better or worse. And in the quiet moments we share with them, they bring home the power of the present.

One cold, rainy winter night several years ago, I realized at 3 a.m. that I had left my cat outside. I scurried downstairs, opened the front door, and found her sitting quietly on the front stoop, wet and cold. I towel-dried her, and five minutes later she was snug, warm and asleep beside me in bed. I compared her response to how a human might react: There was no drama ("It's about time you opened the door. I'm freezing!"); no guilt-tripping ("What in the world were you thinking, leaving me out there?"); no retaliation ("You can forget about snuggling with me after that little escapade!"). She did not waste her time on the past or the future; the present moment was too valuable to miss.

We live in a perfect world, with blessings so deep and vast they are almost too much to take in. Marianne Williamson was right when she said it is our light that frightens us most; this bright, amazing, beautiful, wondrous, incomprehensible universe can seem too good to be true.

And yet, it *is* true. When we realize that, and awaken to it, there is no wanting, no craving, no need to attract more. We are truly basking in the divine, a moment at a time.

The law of attraction can help us improve the circumstances of our lives and is valuable for doing so. The risk is if we begin to believe this is all there is. Our ego is perfectly capable of conjuring up one thing after another that it thinks we "need" in order to be happy. We then find ourselves on the same treadmill that has led so many people to live, in Thoreau's words, "lives of quiet desperation," always chasing after the next thing.

By contrast, the law of attention implies a peaceful practice and expanded awareness. Attention is a manifestation of love, so being more attentive means being more loving. We know this from our own experience: When someone pays attention to us—looking, listening, giving—we feel cared about. Conversely, when someone ignores us, we feel demeaned, insignificant, unloved.

The more we focus on the present, the more we experience "the peace that passes all understanding," and the more ably we radiate that peace to others. The kingdom is at hand; the true riches of life are already here. As we release our need to own, to get and to have, we can apply the power of attention to discover the true bliss that comes from no-self and no-thing at all.

Can I Get a Witness?

REV. KRISTIN RENÉE POWELL

*"As we notice our thoughts and feelings,
we create a disconnect that allows us
to no longer identify with them."*

We all long for the reassurance that our time on the
planet makes a difference and that someone, at least one
other person, can attest to the impact of our lives. Such a witness, usually a dear friend, notices how we have changed and
grown. He or she celebrates our triumphs and spiritual break-
throughs. And these witnesses do not judge! They simply
reflect back to us what they see and hear us doing and saying.

The witnesses of our lives gently point out our mis-
alignments—the places where our words and actions don't
align—and still remain stalwart partners on our journey.
These dear ones observe and celebrate the wonderful manifestations in our lives, such as meaningful work, loving relationships and dreams fulfilled. They remember, for example,

159

that we said we were praying for a life partner and then they watch with delight as the seemingly perfect match appears. At such times, they witness the fulfillment of the law of attraction, or what Unity calls the *law of mind action,* which says thoughts held in mind produce like circumstances in our lives.

While other people can have great capacity to witness and share our joys and challenges, they do not see what is going on inside us. This is a view only we can see—from the inside out.

To apply the law of attraction to realize our highest good, we must begin by doing our inner work. It is first an inside job. When we engage the witness within—when we become observers in our own lives—we not only see outcomes, we know what's happening on the inside, in the invisible world.

The witness inside does not sit in a place of judgment; it merely observes. And because the inner observer is egoless Spirit, it will never derail or disappoint us. The inner witness can lead us to greater fulfillment in our outer lives and, more important, it can expedite our journey to the expansive peace and possibility within us.

Developing our witnessing skills begins at our growing edge—awareness.

Here are three simple steps we can take to become better witnesses to our own lives:

1. **Notice thoughts.**

When we pay attention to our most repetitive and frequent thoughts, the ones we *hold in mind,* we get a preview of what is likely to manifest in our lives.

When we notice our minds taking us out of the current moment and into the future or back to the past, we can redirect our attention to the present.

When we become practiced at watching our thoughts, we can catch our minds before they board the train of thought headed for a wreck. These are the downward-spiraling thoughts that build on one another, draining our life energy and prompting destructive feelings about ourselves.

2. Pay attention to what results.

Empowering and inspiring thoughts lead to life experiences that empower and inspire us. The inner witness notices which thoughts precede pleasing circumstances and which don't.

3. Notice feelings and consciously feel them.

Feelings can be a gateway to wisdom if we allow our objective inner witness to pay attention to them. Once we notice a feeling, we can leave the witness position for a moment to go deeper into the feeling. Then we can shift back to observing and notice where the feeling shows up in our bodies. Our bodies and emotions will reveal a statement in the feeling that implies our thoughts. We only need to listen.

For example, Fred hears on Monday that it might snow on Friday. He feels tense for several days, but he doesn't know why. Finally, Fred checks in and witnesses his feelings. "Hmmm, there is fear here. I have a sinking feeling in my solar plexus." Then he listens for a statement in the feeling. What emerges is: "I am afraid it will snow this week and that I will have an accident. If it snows when I'm at work, I might have an accident." This is the persistent thought (held in mind) that is creating the feelings of fear and tension in Fred.

Now he has the power to change the thought. It

could become: "Bad weather has no power over me. I will find alternate transportation if it snows. I am safe." As he changes his thoughts, the feeling eases and the constriction in his body subsides. Now Fred's body feels soft and open as thoughts of safety and peace of mind prevail.

If we continue to identify with our thoughts and feelings (as Fred initially did), we can lose our conscious, spiritual perspective. As we notice our thoughts and feelings, we create a disconnect that allows us to no longer identify with them. Instead, we begin to know ourselves as the witness. The inner witness, like a dear friend, reflects back the thoughts and feelings it has observed. We can then direct the mind to release life-draining thoughts and adopt life-affirming thoughts such as:

I am whole and healthy.

I am one with Divine Mind and therefore guided to make wise decisions.

I am always safe in the presence of God.

It all starts with awareness, and awareness is heightened through witnessing.

A great way to practice witnessing is during meditation. Take some time apart and sit still. Consciously breathe and ask, What is happening within me right now? Then shift into being the witness and observe. When we take time apart to practice, it is easier to activate the inner witness during the day, especially when a challenge arises.

While friends who serve as witnesses are wonderful gifts in our lives, they come and go, just as people come and go in the physical realm. By contrast, the inner witness is more like the presence of Spirit—always with us and always available to us. We enter that presence when we witness the way we co-create our lives through our thoughts.

Can you get a witness? Yes, you already have one. Turn within and you will find it. Practice the few simple steps above and witness yourself becoming a freer, more peaceful and joyful being than you ever imagined possible.

Nothing and No One Is Against You

REV. GARY SIMMONS, TH.D.

*"Without exception, when your life looks and feels
against you, you are being who you are not.
You have confused your being with your having."*

It is impossible to experience abundance in your life,
harmony in relationships, and inner well-being if you believe
that something or someone is against you. Until you realize
that the entire universe is for you, you may never experience
your wholeness and true worth—the secret to abundance
and peace of mind.

All unhappiness, lack and personal suffering are
caused by confusing your self with what you have. What you
have is not you.

Several years ago after my first book, *The I of the Storm*, was published, my then wife, Nan, was diagnosed with terminal brain cancer. The book's primary theme is *nothing and no one is against you.* When Nan read these words she threw the book at me and said, "This is a bunch of crap! How can you say that nothing is against me, when this cancer is killing me?" Later, she began to realize that, while her body was dying, she was not her body. Her body had cancer, but she was not her body, and therefore, she would not let herself be diminished by the experience of having a dying body. She became filled with gratitude for each moment and felt blessed by the company of family and friends who attended to her needs. She used her remaining months to enjoy the experiences she otherwise took for granted. Her prayers for healing took the form of self-acceptance, forgiveness and inner peace. She reconciled with her former husband and discovered a strength of being that moved her loved ones to tears. Her resolve to find wholeness took her beyond her body and into the richness of her own heart. People were drawn to be in her presence. Near the end, she became luminous, and in spite of the debilitating effects of the disease, she was lucid and present. Her passing was peaceful, pain-free and dignified.

While she could have easily chosen to make her dying body an enemy, and the prospect of an untimely passing a cruel ordeal, she worked through her denial, anger, sadness and regret and discovered that her essence was not eclipsed by her life situation. She saw that her life and her life situation were entirely different, yet interconnected and mutually beneficial dynamics of being. She had cancer, but she was not her cancer. She would use her cancer to heal her soul. Her body would die, but she would live on. Her choice to not confuse herself with her experience freed her from what could have been an otherwise agonizing process common among those who contract this disease. Instead, her realization became her healing and my healing, and the abundance her loved ones and family never expected to receive.

Whatever you have as your situation, experience or circumstance, it is not you. You are not your things. You are not your story. You are not your body. You are not your thoughts or feelings. You have things, but they are not you. If you confuse your *self* with what you have—when you believe that you are your things, your story, your body or your thoughts and feelings—your identity is entangled in what you have. And because everything that you have is impermanent and subject to change in an instant, any confusion between *being* and *having* will ultimately result in disappointment or lack. When you confuse your essence with what you have or don't have, you become impoverished and driven by external circumstances.

To expose this incongruence—*having equals being*—your life will sometimes look and feel as if it is against you. But your life is not against you, it is against *who you are not*. Interpersonal difficulties, turmoil, lack or misfortunes are symptomatic of being *who you are not* instead of being who you truly are—the whole and perfect expression of God. When you relate from your real self, it is impossible to feel diminished. When you are lost, however, in what you have or being *who you are not*, someone or something will appear to be against you. But the situation or person is not against you, it is a mirror unto your own disconnect from your true self; it is against your confusion or against your incongruence—the things that you mistake for yourself.

You may have beliefs or feelings of unworthiness, but your unworthiness is not you. If you are capable of confusing yourself with your unworthiness, you will attract into your life the perfect situation that will be a mirror unto your unworthiness. Life, the Universe, Spirit, the Divine, cannot allow you to become completely lost and asleep in *who you are not* without there being a mechanism by which you can recover from this confusion.

Since what you *have* is not you, you can free yourself from anxiety, stress and even suffering during those occasions when you do not have what you want or when you have something in your life be against you. If, in the having or the not having of something, your sense of well-being and worth is affected, you are no longer functioning from your spiritual identity—your real self. The experience of having something *has* you. Your sense of "I," your *being*, becomes entangled in what is *me*, *my* and *mine*.

Spiritual teachers have long since made the distinction between the real self and the ego—*who you are not*—and the trouble that befalls the person when the two are confused. The first step to recovery is to catch yourself *being* who you are not or confusing yourself with your experience—seeing the relationship between who you are being and what you are having as your life experience. Think of your real self as the animating force, and what you *have*, such as your thoughts or your body or your car or your relationship or even your story, as what your essence uses to fulfill its purpose. A false self arises when you no longer recognize yourself as the essence out of which meaning, relevance and value arise. Instead, you mistake what you have for who you are. This *disconnect* from the chain and sequence of *being* as it expresses itself as the *presence* of your life causes a bifurcation of perception where the mechanism of *seeing* becomes a surrogate selfhood and self-system. Seeing becomes a form of *I-entification*—a superimposing of identity (me, my, mine) onto one's experience. You become conditioned to look to what you have as a reflection of yourself instead of the light source that gives what you have its substance. And while this impairment of perception is very problematic, it is effectively dealt with by retraining how you see—seeing yourself and your relationship to your experience as two interrelated phenomena.

Who do you have to *be* to have someone or something against you? You have to be *who you are not*—unworthy, inadequate, afraid. When someone judges you and you become defensive, who do you have to be in order to BE defensive? Who do you have to be in order to have the experience of lack in your life? Who do you have to be in order to have something be the matter with you? Without exception, when your life looks and feels against you, you are being *who you are not*. You have confused your *being* with your *having*.

You can free yourself from the drama of life and attract abundant good when you bring awareness to your experience and see how it is a reflection of who you are being. By embracing the present moment completely, with gratitude and curiosity, you allow yourself to see beyond the situation and into the field of infinite possibilities. Regardless of how the present moment looks and feels, it receives its life and light from your presence. When your *being* is eclipsed by a false sense of self, you can correct this dynamic by simply being present without resistance or commentary. The moment-by-moment embrace of any situation will eventually bring forth the distinction between *you* and what you are *having* as your experience. If the situation looks and feels against you, the situation is exposing your own incongruence. You have caught yourself being *who you are not*.

The next time you feel uneasy or anxious, ask yourself, Who am I *being* right now? Begin to see the relationship between *who you are being* and the quality of your life experience. Next, see how the unpleasant quality of your experience is really a mirror to that part of yourself that is not connected to your own sense of well-being and worth—that *had* you been connected, you could be in the experience without feeling diminished by it. Once you establish the practice of asking yourself, Who do I have to *be* in order to have this experience?, you will gradually refrain from making your experience against you. In a few short weeks this practice will yield life-transforming results. You will catch yourself in the moment making someone responsible for your experience. You will find yourself enjoying greater peace and less stress because your attention stays present and your awareness focused on how every situation and experience is for you. With this frame of mind and attitude of heart you will become a magnet for abundant good to flow into your life. By seeing that you are not your experience, that you have experiences, but experiences do not have you, you can *use* your experience to enhance what you have. Nothing and no one is against you. This is the *secret* that is beyond the Secret.

Powerful Beyond Measure

REV. JAMES TRAPP

"The great metaphysical law is that
we get to keep everything we give away."

The truth implied by the law of attraction is that each one of us is powerful beyond measure.

God potential is in each of us. We call this power within the Christ presence, the Buddhic mind, the God within us, our divinity—nearer than breathing, closer than hands and feet, that which cannot be hurt, harmed, hindered or endangered in any way, shape or form. This power and potential in us is always seeking to be expressed and released. Nothing can stop it, regardless of what is happening in the external world. We can, however, direct this force, which gives us enormous power and enormous responsibility.

This teaching is not about waiting for a Messiah or great teacher to come back to save us. It is not about waiting for external conditions to change before we begin to live the God life. It is not about other people changing before we express the presence of God. This teaching is about activating and expressing that which is within us already, beginning to shine that which is within us, so that Heaven—ever-expanding good—may be evidenced through us and by us.

How do we activate this God presence to contribute to Heaven on earth and live a full, satisfying life? It begins with the law of giving.

In Luke 6:38, the master teacher, Jesus Christ, reminds us, "Give and it shall be given to you ... pressed down, shaken together, running over."

Our giving is an articulation of a spiritual law. The creative flow in us is a giving process. Our act of giving does not change God, causing some sort of anthropomorphic being to sit up and take notice and give us something back in return. Rather, we're giving way to a process. Giving is an aspect of the infinite that is inherent in all of life. It is like the process of inhaling and exhaling. It is a cycle of receiving and giving.

Sometimes people say, "I've given and given and given. I just can't give anymore. There's nothing happening in my life. I feel depleted, exhausted, unappreciated, unrecognized. I just can't give any more." This is an indication that the individual is not giving aright. The individual has been caught up in the belief of separation—a belief that they have their own resources from which to give, their own stash, their own private personal reserve, separate and apart from

God. They believe if they give of this stash, God will bless them and give them more recognition, more money, more prestige, a better job, whatever.

But the truth is, we have no private stash. We are often acculturated into a materialism that sees us as separate from our source, from God, from life itself—separate from the infinite. This thinking leads to depletion, exhaustion, anger, frustration, jealousy, envy and competition. And appearances in the world begin to give evidence to that.

We must ultimately come to the realization that the earth is the Lord's, and what we are giving, God has already given us. We are points for its fulfillment. Either we're in the flow of this giving, this magnificence moving through us according to our own consciousness, or we're not in the flow, and we're either giving and becoming exhausted, or we're not giving at all. To get in the flow of true giving, we must give with the right motivation—not for a reward, but because it is our nature as spiritual beings.

We are here to radiate the spiritual presence of God and to give without looking for a reward because that is our natural being. Those who throw stones at us, talk about us, criticize us—we give them more love, more peace, more harmony. Those who shoot negativity at us, they go right to the top of the prayer list.

In August I went to Chucky Cheese with my son Jaelan. There was a young girl there who was at a ride, and she didn't have any money or any tokens. So Jaelan just gave her a token, and she took the ride. A few minutes later, the young girl tracked him down and gave him the coupons she had collected as a result of going on that ride.

When we begin to practice the spiritual laws, goodness and mercy will track us down to give us our own good in
life. The great metaphysical law is that we get to keep everything we give away. Imelda Shanklin, in her book *What Are
You?*, says "Never want for another person what you would
not want to see objectified in your own life." Whatever we
want in our life, let even our so-called worst enemy have it
and know there is no separation, that we keep everything we
give away. This is how the law of circulation works.

Ecclesiastes 11:1 says "Cast your bread upon the
waters. In a short period of time, it will return unto you." We
must ask ourselves, "What bread have I cast upon the waters
lately? What have I circulated?" People say, "My good is not
coming. Nothing is happening." We must ask, "What have
you circulated lately?" Because we only get back what we
cast and nothing else.

Metaphysically, bread means universal substance. And
water equals the sea of infinite possibilities, infinite potential.
We are to cast our bread on the infinite possibility daily, and
what we cast returns to us multiplied, pressed down, shaken
together and running over. If we do not cast any bread, we
do not get any. If we do not cast love, we do not get love. If
we don't cast emanation of peace, we do not get emanation
of peace. This is a universal law. We are either circulating or
stagnating. It's up to us.

What have you placed upon the waters lately? Where
have you withheld a kind word, compassion, forgiveness?
Where have you withheld your self?

Ralph Waldo Emerson reminds us that when you
give, you put the universe in your debt. The universe then

has to balance the ledger to push you to another level of self-expression. When you give more than you're temporarily compensated for, either the space for you will expand or you will expand beyond your space. But if we're in "sick and tired" consciousness, we will not be able to handle the higher energy that wants to express through us and as us. If we fully occupy and appreciate where we are, envisioning what we want in our life, we cannot help but advance to a higher level of expression.

We must find an outlet to express, to shine our gifts, to share our talents, and to utilize our time. We have to say, "I'm here to be a rushing river, flowing downhill. There is not only a strong inlet of Spirit moving through me, but there is a strong outlet. I must be a giver in life, a contributor." We must wake up every day and say "How can I give more of myself to life today?" Then something comes back to us, and we'll never be stagnant—we'll never be a swamp. We'll be an ocean. We'll be a wave on that ocean, flowing with the expression of pure spirit. We will be individuals in control of the reservoir of energy that needs an opening to flow through. This is our destiny.

We are a conscious life form, expressing the power and the presence and the love of God. We are a universe in miniature. There is a power here—a love, a capacity to give, a capacity to shine, and divine creativity—right here. You're it. You are the power you are seeking, the love you are trying to get. When you wake up to that, you will be part of the great ecstatic dance of the universe that says "I am the delight of God, brought up with the creations of the world." Before anything was even manifested, you were already the delight of God because you are an infinite possibility for God to express itself. The spirit of the living God is saying, "Tag, you're it! I need you to express more of me in this dimension." This is your life. This is what we are about.

Second Timothy tells us God did not give us a spirit of fear but a spirit of power and love and a sound mind. As we make this the activity of our consciousness, we watch the mountains of seeming impossibility crumble. We step up to our infinite potential and demonstrate we are powerful beyond measure as we allow that power to flow through us by our giving. We let go of excuses and recognize there is something within us waiting to be expressed, to shine, radiate, glow and transform our lives and the world in which we live.

There is within us a power greater than anything that is in the world. It has been given to us from the spirit of the living God. We release any blockages or hindrances so that we can be what we are here to be.

The Law of Wholeness: You Are Magnificent!

RIMA E. BONARIO

*"When we know we are a divine expression
of the Most High, our life becomes
the greatest song we can ever sing."*

It is wonderful that the recent attention given to the law of attraction is allowing so many people to learn that they can be released from the toxicity of victim thinking and the life of misery it consciously or unconsciously creates. For students of Unity and New Thought Christianity, the law of attraction is not new. In fact, it is one of the five basic Unity teachings. Principle number three speaks specifically to the law of attraction, and principles four and five refer to how we put it into action. Here, in my own words, are the basic concepts:

1. God is the source and creator of all. There is no other enduring power. God is good and present everywhere.

2. We are spiritual beings, created in God's image. The spirit of God lives within each person; therefore, all people are inherently good.

3. We create our life experiences through our way of thinking.

4. There is power in affirmative prayer, which we believe increases our connection to God.

5. Knowledge of these spiritual principles is not enough. We must live them.

The law of attraction is a very rich and deep teaching, with many subtleties that are important to understand in order to create a life of joy. It takes conscious effort to pay attention to the kinds of thoughts that permeate our thinking and our speech. If we set our intention to listen to our inner and outer dialogue, it will not take long for us to spot patterns of thought that focus on the very things we do not want.

For example, the thought "There isn't enough money to cover the bills" brings about a continuation of that experience. The thought "I need more money" creates more need. Even a thought like "I hope I have more money soon" reinforces a state of lack in the now. We change our future circumstances when we think thoughts of abundance, such as "My life is abundant. My every desire is fulfilled. I prosper and enjoy sharing my prosperity with others." You can substitute the theme of relationship, career, health, global circumstances or any other area of life you wish to change.

Yet simply saying these things as affirmations may not bring them into existence. Affirmations are good as an exercise to help you build and strengthen your "thinking muscles," but without the feelings associated with those thoughts, they fall flat. By focusing on what it would feel like to have, be or do whatever it is you desire, you begin to draw that into your life. In recent conversations about the law of attraction, all sorts of practical techniques are offered to help you focus your thoughts and feelings. Investing time daily in these techniques is helpful. Unfortunately, most people spend their days stuck in their habitual patterns of thinking and feeling that focus on what they do not have or worrying about how and when what they want will appear.

Why is it so hard for us to make real and lasting change in our thinking and feeling patterns? Perhaps the answer lies in the impossible task of consciously directing every thought or feeling you have in a single day. Despite whatever time and effort you put into specific techniques, it is your unconscious beliefs that produce the vast majority of your thoughts and feelings which draw to you experiences that create more of those same thoughts and feelings.

Changing our habitual thinking can happen only when we change our beliefs. We must actively uncover and examine our conscious and unconscious beliefs which are at the core of our patterns of thought and feeling. You can make a decision to change them and then reinforce that change with aligned thoughts and feelings.

One of the most damaging beliefs our society holds is that of the sinful nature of humanity. I believe there is a reason why the law of attraction appears as the third and not the first of Unity's basic teachings. Before we can effectively use the law of attraction, we must understand and live from what I call *the law of wholeness*.

Think of it this way: The law of attraction is the vehicle of your life and the law of wholeness is the steering wheel that allows you to decide where you go. What good is a vehicle to you if you can't control where it takes you?

The law of wholeness is simply this: Humans, and human consciousness, are a creation of and exist within the sacred wholeness of God, the One Presence and One Power; therefore you are sacred and whole (see Unity principles one and two).

Imagine you begin a practice of thinking about all the good things you desire. You even allow yourself to feel the feelings of success. But what if at the core of your self-identity sits the belief that you are unworthy of such good or that you are broken or lost and will never have or be anything good unless you are fixed by some outside force? What if you think that suffering actually makes you a better, more pious and holy person? What if you believe your very existence is an offense to God?

If these ideas form the basis of your belief system, consciously or unconsciously, you will naturally manifest a life that is to be endured rather than enjoyed. If you do not see that you are born of wholeness, that the sacred is in you and you are in the sacred, you cannot create a life that reflects sacred wholeness.

The personal experience of many of us has borne this out. So, too, have the lives of mystics, saints, profits, sages and holy men and women of the ages. Their examples prove that it is through the understanding and experience of wholeness, of oneness with the Divine, that we find joy. By embracing our inherent wholeness and divine heritage, we find our true nature. When we know we are a divine expression of the Most High, our life becomes the greatest song we can ever sing. Creating a life that manifests the endless blessings of oneness with the Divine becomes the point of life. No longer is there any need to search for meaning.

Many traditional Christians resist the concept of wholeness and the law of attraction often because they seem to challenge doctrine and dogma that have grown up around Scripture. Or worse, they seem to challenge the scripture itself. Yet the Bible is replete with evidence of the spiritual truth of wholeness. In his book *Glimpses of Truth,* Thomas Shepherd writes, "A fresh look at the Bible shows very few passages which mutter about the dark side of humanity but a lot of verses, chapters and whole books proclaiming creation's wholeness before God."

The real conflict is not with Scripture or the teachings of Christ, but with the fifth-century perspective of St. Augustine's assertion that we are "fallen," defective and stained. Again, Shepherd writes, "Augustine pushed for a nonbiblical fall-and-redemption Christianity based on his dualistic, pessimistic, Manachean background. In a fall-and-redemption centered religion, humans 'fell' from some kind of pristine goodness to a state of brokenness. Humanity wallows in its fallen state, sinful and lost, until a divine agent cleanses and restores us to wholeness and harmony with God."

Most Christians, practicing and nonpracticing, would recognize this line of thinking. Many would agree with it as truth. Many more continue to be consciously and unconsciously influenced by it as it is at the very core of western religious and societal thought. We can see examples of humans living up (or down) to this expectation every day. This is the law of attraction working unconsciously, without a steering wheel—the law of wholeness.

When we allow ourselves to see the Divine everywhere, and believe that there is nowhere God is not—including inside us—we can release any sense of unworthiness and embrace our magnificence. With the understanding of our magnificence come the right to a life of joy *and* the responsibility to live from and fully express this magnificence.

Imagine a world filled with humans who are conscious of their wholeness and who identify with and make choices from their divine nature. Imagine the good, the joy, the love and the caring that will be poured out across the planet when all humans openly embrace and fully express their sacred selves. Just imagine it!

Is there any better use for the law of attraction, guided by the law of wholeness, than to manifest humanity living up to its divine heritage? It can be done, with each of us opening to and accepting our wholeness, one person at a time.

Why not start with you? Why not start now? Believe it. Imagine it. Feel it. It is so.

The Secret of the Bicycle Wheel

Rev. Phillip M. Pierson

*"You are a limitless mind-being
with 12 wonderful faculties within you."*

Did you know that you can't have a bicycle wheel that doesn't have at least 12 spokes? You can have one with less but it won't run true and will in time face total collapse. I am not an expert in wheels, but I share this on the authority of none other than Buckminster Fuller, who was, according to many, the Michelangelo of the twentieth century. In his book *Synergetics*, he said, "Nature coordinates in 12 alternatively equi-economical degrees of freedom—six positive and six negative. For this reason, 12 is the minimum number of spokes you must have in a wire wheel in order to make a comprehensive structural integrity of that tool. You must have six positive and six negative spokes to offset all polar or equatorial diaphragming and torque." Fuller was a master at the geometric building blocks of our physical world. He also said that whatever is true physically is true metaphysically, which precedes all manifestation.

This leads us to the even greater secret that is behind the secret of the bicycle wheel. It is the metaphysical reality behind the appearance of our physical lives. It is a secret that is told symbolically in the Old Testament (a scripture for the Jewish, Muslim and Christian faiths). It was a Truth that was intuitively received by the authors of some of the Old Testament. That Truth, that secret, is that we as mind-beings—our metaphysical selves—have essentially 12 attributes. They are faculties of mind that are essential to our wholeness. We can, and usually do, run on less. To run true and to live everlastingly, however, we must learn to function fully and consciously with all of our faculties. Like the spokes of a bike they must be present (in our awareness), they must be taut (used), and they must be balanced.

The Old Testament contains many references to the number 12, but most notably in the central story of the 12 sons of Jacob and the founding of the 12 tribes of Israel. While there may be some historical evidence for this tale, it is clearly meant to be a symbolic presentation of the essential attributes of humankind as mind-beings. Jesus was well aware of this symbolism when he chose 12 disciples and referred to "lifting them up."

What this means is that until we recognize ourselves as mind-beings (spiritual beings) made up of 12 faculties of mind, we can never "run true" to what God intends us to be. *The Secret* has called the world's attention to the exciting knowledge that you can attract into your life the things and results you desire by believing and seeing it. This can often be demonstrated, and the world needs to know it because so many of us use it in reverse. That is, we believe and see negative possibilities and attract them to us. But there are many skeptics who point out with authority the many examples of people who apparently believed in the right manner and still didn't get the results they desired. Is "The Secret" not real? It's real, but it is only two spokes on the wheel. Used to the neglect of the other 10 spokes results in at best a wobbly wheel (life) or at worst, failure.

"The Secret" is based on two of our mind faculties. Metaphysically we refer to them as "faith" and "imagination." Faith is the perceiving faculty of mind. It is what we perceive to be true (real). Imagination is its companion faculty as it perceives in the form of pictures. Imagination gives shape and form to our perceptions of reality. These two faculties are functioning in all of us constantly. "The Secret" calls us to be conscious of their manifesting power and to direct them toward positive results only. But "The Secret" leaves out the other 10 faculties that are present in us and must be used and balanced with faith and imagination to get a good and heavenly life. The other faculties are will, understanding, zeal, dominion, love, wisdom, order, strength, renunciation and life. The secret of the bicycle is that each of these faculties is within us and must be consciously developed—made taut—and balanced with all the others.

It is a lifetime (actually many lifetimes) study to do this, but it begins with awareness. Let me just give you one example of how this works in regard to "The Secret." If you do learn to use your faith and imagination to attract to you money, fame and romance and neglect the pivotal faculty of all, *love,* you will find that none of your gains bring you happiness at all. You will wobble through your life in the emptiness that we see in the lives of so many people who have failed to see that love must be pivotal in their lives if they are to find happiness. And while love is pivotal, *all* the other faculties are essential to know the true potential we have for living as demonstrated by Jesus Christ and to a degree by many others.

So let the bicycle wheel be a constant reminder to you of the miracle of how God has created you. You are a limitless mind-being with 12 wonderful faculties within you. To use these faculties rightly and in a balanced manner is to roll through life in a heavenly manner and to know the life that God meant for you to have. That's the promise of the secret of the bicycle wheel!

Setting a Trap for Gratitude

REV. RUTH WALLACE

*"Practice gratitude daily and your life will change
in ways you can hardly imagine."*

Gratitude, like the law of attraction, is one of the
most powerful forces in the universe. When we feel gratitude, we feel love, joy, appreciation, humility and peace. We
also attract even more experiences into our lives for which to
feel grateful.

Some people believe God is constantly sending abundance to us, but the truth is, God *is* the abundance. When
we ask for something, we are simply tapping into that abundance. It is not our job to manifest abundance; it is our job to
demonstrate our abundance, by understanding that God *is* the
abundance we seek.

Gratitude attracts greater abundance and has wonderful effects on us. When I am grateful, I feel light. I am able to be present. I forget about the little things—and even the big things—I worry about. I feel peaceful. I am not thinking about myself, but am "outwardly" focused. I see what's around me. I can sit quietly and watch nature. I can observe the birds and the flowers. They attract my attention, and I am grateful that I see them. My gratitude brings still more peace and awareness, and the upward spiral continues. My heart opens. I am happy and filled with joy. I watch the sky and the clouds and see them changing. Sitting by the ocean, I watch the sailboats and the birds as they dive for food. The world seems ethereal. I am one with God and all is well.

Gratitude brings me into conscious contact with God. When I become grateful, my body chemistry changes. I appreciate my life and all the people in it. I am grateful for my close and supportive relationships, for my loving relationship with each of my granddaughters, for my closeness to my friends and colleagues. Even as I write this, my heart sings.

When we feel gratitude, our faces shine and our eyes brighten. Others are attracted to us. When we feel grateful, we see God in everything and everyone. We are kinder, gentler and more compassionate. We find the right words to say to help others.

When we're grateful, we create an ontological space that is safe; a space filled with grace, peace, love and joy. We are safe to be around; we are fun to be around. Thus, we attract more safety, more beauty, more love and more fun. We make wonderful spiritual connections with people because we are present to the God-essence in them.

When we are grateful, we are present to everything in our lives. We are grateful for it all because we see God in it all.

Too often we think of gratitude as the *result* of something. Someone does something nice for us, and we feel grateful. That is *passive* gratitude. I am advocating *active* gratitude. Conscious gratitude. Active gratitude is a way of living, a way of *being*. When we choose active gratitude, we are choosing to change our energy. We are using the law of attraction to bring to us more love, more good health and more abundance. We are co-creating our life with God.

One way to feel more gratitude is through prayer. Ask God to show you how to trust. Ask God to show you how to create a loving relationship with a power greater than yourself. Pray yourself into a relationship with God that will comfort you, bless you and sustain you. Allow God to love and bless you. Allow yourself to become aware of your good. By becoming aware of our good, we begin the upward spiral of gratitude.

As you begin a gratitude practice, you will be guided to the next logical step. Unity co-founder Charles Fillmore said, "Pray and move your feet." If we don't take the action we are guided to take, we are doing nothing but magical thinking. Nothing happens in life until we make a commitment. Infuse your mind with your vision. Commit to see your blessings and feel grateful for them.

One way to tap the power of gratitude is by keeping a gratitude journal. Get a notebook, and before you to go bed each night, write down 10 things for which you are grateful. They might be as simple as "I woke up." We take so many things for granted each day. This exercise helps us remember how truly beautiful the world is and how God works in our lives each day.

Most of us focus on the 10 percent of our lives that make us unhappy instead of the 90 percent for which we are grateful. Try reversing that. List at least 10 things from the 90 percent you are grateful for under the following headings: Health, Material Possessions, Relationships, Personal and Spiritual Growth and Creative Expression. By focusing on these, you enact the law of attraction and begin drawing to you even more good.

Then look at the 10 percent of your life that includes the "problem" areas—the things you want to change. Write them down, but instead of seeing them as problems, look for the blessings in them. If you can't see the good, then ask or, if necessary, *demand* to see the blessing. This is what Jacob did when he wrestled with the angel of God. He wouldn't let the angel go until he got a blessing. You can do the same. As you begin to see the blessing in each "problem" area, write the blessings down. You'll be surprised at how many you find.

For journal writing, I recommend the three-page approach: Get a pencil and three sheets of clean paper. Sit in a quiet place and get centered. Turn on soft music if you like. When you feel ready, begin writing the things you are grateful for and how you feel as you write them down. Don't stop writing until the three pages are filled. By the time you finish, you will experience the *power* of gratitude.

Practice gratitude daily and your life will change in ways you can hardly imagine. Discover the beautiful life you already have, right here and now!

The Sower

REV. DUKE TUFTY

*"If we truly want our lives to change for the better,
if we want to express a greater degree of our potential,
we have to commit 100 percent of our time, energy and focus."*

Throughout the ages, the great thinkers, philosophers and spiritual masters have talked about a higher realm of awareness within us—a state of mind, a way of thinking, a type of perception—where we experience the ultimate sense of well-being. The Buddhists call this higher realm of awareness Nirvana. They describe it as being like a gentle breeze that finds all things worthy of caress. The Hindus consider this awareness a mystical union with Brahman, their chief God. The Zoroastrians call it paradise, and they say the loveliest becomes lovelier.

Jesus referred to it as the Kingdom of Heaven, and He said it is accessible to every person—here and now. His entire ministry was based on the Kingdom of Heaven. Every parable is a Kingdom of Heaven parable. He had discovered an awareness within Him that greatly enriched the living experience, and His only goal, His primary objective, was to teach others to do the same. Jesus didn't see Himself as the exception, but as an example.

He said, "What I have done you can do also." The Kingdom of Heaven is within you.

The gospels were originally written in Greek, in which the word *kingdom* means realm. The word *heaven* means a process of rising up to higher levels of happiness and empowerment. So the Kingdom of Heaven translates as a higher realm of awareness within us, characterized by greater degrees of happiness and empowerment.

The 30 parables of the New Testament are put forth in a particular sequence so they become like stepping-stones on a secret pathway that leads to a deeper state of well-being and personal evolution.

But shortly after embarking on his ministry, after teaching the first three parables, Jesus realized something was wrong. The people weren't catching on; they weren't getting it. So the fourth parable was his response to the problem. It is the parable of the sower, and is often called the key that unlocks the deeper level of meaning in all the other parables.

In the parable, Jesus tells of a farmer who went out to plant seeds so he could harvest a bountiful crop. As he scattered the seeds, some fell on the road and the birds swept down and ate them up. Some fell on a flat rock and they had no place to put down roots. Some fell in the weeds and as they came up, the weeds suffocated them and crowded them out. And some fell on good earth and produced a bountiful crop.

We are like the farmer in the parable. Instead of creating a field full of crops, we are creating our lives. The seeds represent our potential. We have the potential to become more, to live better, to be happier, to love more. And just as the seeds need to be planted in good soil, nurtured and tended to in order to grow, our potential is totally dependent on the thoughts we think. Positive thoughts nurture our potential, and we get positive results.

So here lies the problem in the parable of the sower. Some seeds fall on the roadside and the birds take them away. Some seeds fall on a rock and they can't take root. And some seeds land in the weeds and the sprouts get smothered out. Seventy-five percent of the farmer's efforts are wasted because he is not paying attention, he is not focused, he is not truly committed to what he is doing.

And so it is with us at times. We hear the good news about the potential we have to change our lives in many positive ways, but we don't really set our intention, our unwavering intention to commit to that process, so what we hear is like the seeds carried off by the birds. Or we allow the negative attitudes of the past to continue and dominate, so new thoughts can't take root, like the seeds that landed on the rock. Or we let the attitudes of others smother out the new thoughts and they can't grow, like the seeds that landed in the weeds.

One of the reasons that 12-step programs are so successful is that they address these three problems for recovering addicts. First and foremost, it is recommended they attend 90 meetings in 90 days—that's commitment. Second, they have to engage in the implementation of the 12 steps—each of which moves them away from their negative attitudes, heals situations of the past and strongly plants within them positive attitudes. Third, the program suggests the person find a new playground with new playmates. The chances of a recovering alcoholic staying sober while continuing to hang around with his drinking buddies at the local tavern are nil.

The program works because the members are committed. They work the program, and they find healthy environments and healthy social circles to be a part of.

The parable of the sower tells us three things. First, if we truly want our lives to change for the better, if we want to express a greater degree of our potential, we have to commit 100 percent of our time, energy and focus. Second, we have to become aware when old, negative, defeating ways of thinking surface and do what psychologists call a *pattern interrupt*. We interrupt the pattern of negative thinking by putting our attention back on our intention. And third, we need to spend our time in a positive environment with positive people, doing positive things.

To some this might seem like a lot of work. You might even wonder if it is worth the effort. But in truth, it is much, much harder to live in an unsatisfactory way, with a low sense of well-being or an unsettling notion that there is more to life than what we are experiencing.

Nothing brings intensity, satisfaction, meaning, pleasure, passion and fulfillment like your life becoming more than it has ever been.

Jesus' message in this parable is simple and to the point. If we want to make positive changes in our lives, we have to set our intention and be determined that is what is going to happen. The power is ours.

The Secretless Universe

REV. MICHAEL BERNARD BECKWITH

*"Wherever you are in the spiritual continuum
of consciousness, just say 'Yes' to it,
enter it fully, so that you may be ushered into
the next step in your unfoldment."*

In truth, the Universe has absolutely no secrets. The full display of its magnificence is available at all times, and it has been so since the dawn of creation. It could be said that the Universe is the ultimate exhibitionist. Experiencing its seeming miracles and understanding its laws are not dependent upon the Universe, for it is not fickle in revealing itself to some and not to others. What is required is that an individual be qualified in consciousness to plummet the depths of the stuff out of which creation is revealed in all its glory. Nothing is secret to those who have the inner eyes to see, the lowly listening to hear, the sensitivity to touch, the cultivated soul to taste the Cosmic Elixir.

Few there are who are sufficiently on fire to sit under the Bodhi tree of their consciousness long enough, disciplined enough, to not move until there remain no obstacles to coming face-to-face with Reality. This is what the Master Teacher, Jesus the Christ, accomplished during his 40 days of seclusion in the desert; it's what the Buddha realized when he became enlightened sitting under the Bodhi tree. Both of these enlightened beings—and others since their time—show us the way.

When considering the secretless Universe, it is important to distinguish secrets from mysteries. The human mind can go only so far. Its sciences and telescopes can only penetrate so far. However, our inner spiritual technology can go all the way from secrets to mysteries. Mysteries are those areas that the human mind cannot reach, simply because it is not the mind's function to do so. It is the spirit-soul that contains what is necessary to reach into the depths of Life's mysteries.

So before you make that reservation in the next available cave in the Himalayas, let's consider how we may start right where we are as we meet the challenges of twenty-first century living. First, it's important not to make excuses for not keeping our daily commitment to meditate, pray, study and serve. This is practical technology to keep us free from the tyranny of trends—a common denominator of our society that becomes the "standard" for measuring our success. Instead, we commit to doing our spiritual practices—both inner and outer—whether we feel like it or not. Feeling like it has nothing to do with whether we do it or not. This cultivates a nonattachment to the fruits of our efforts, which means that we do our practices for their own sake whether we receive immediate results or not. We continue in trust—knowing, offering and surrendering to the Spirit in a state of gratitude for our precious human birth.

Secondly, we practice what I call the three Cs for transformation: conversation, company and commitment. *Conversation* is watching what comes out of our mouths. It is important to understand that our speech carries an energy, a vibration that advertises our state of consciousness. Is what we are saying necessary, kind and true? Are we gossiping, or are we talking about what contributes to the upliftment of our listeners and ourselves? Or are we spewing negativity? Even if our words are "spiritually correct," those who can sense the vibration they carry will know if we are genuine or not. Naturally, there is a time to share those things that weigh heavily upon our hearts, those things that we are working on within ourselves with a trusted confidant, counselor, spiritual teacher or friend. At times we must clear the air and take responsibility to talk with those our words may have hurt. At other times we may be called upon to say things that we know will hurt another for their own good. Conversation may become a bit heated as we endeavor to arrive at an understanding with our loved ones, friends, co-workers, bosses, even within our spiritual community. We're not talking about suppressing or repressing here, but what the Psalmist meant in 141:3 when saying, "Set a guard over my mouth, O Lord; keep watch over the door of my lips." It's the motivation that's important.

Next, it is wise to notice the *company* we keep, not in a judgmental way, but to observe the influence we have upon one another. The great yogi Paramhansa Yogananda said that company is stronger than willpower and, while we clearly see how this pertains to youth, do we see how it applies to us as adults? That is why the Buddha referred to the *sangha*—one's spiritual community—as one of the three jewels. Those with whom we mix are very important to our spiritual practice because they support us on the path, keep us humble, and encourage us when we feel discouraged. Are you keeping company with those who have an affirmative approach to life? How do you perceive the quality of your company? Of course this isn't about being falsely cheerful and positive; it's about being authentic while being sensitive to the vibration of your consciousness, words and presence upon others.

Conversation and company combine with *commitment*. When you become committed to growing, expanding in consciousness, to evolving, you release powerful life energy. Commitment is the fuel that drives your practice, which is fire that transforms consciousness.

At this point it is important to define *consciousness*, because this word is bandied about so often that its true meaning has become diluted. Consciousness is that which makes us aware of the contents of our being. Consciousness is the "watcher," that which is beyond thought, beyond the thinking mind. It is the being of us. We are first and foremost consciousness. Now there are levels of consciousness: superconsciousness, Christ Consciousness and Cosmic Consciousness. We are a living, breathing being of consciousness. Our ability to be aware that we are aware is that nonaction of consciousness. Nonaction because it simply is. Consciousness ushers us into a relationship with the Reality of our being.

We started out talking about the secretless Universe. There is some sort of intrigue that entices us as human beings toward secrets. We sense a magical quality about secrets because there is a nuance that a secret is something special. We even think we become special when someone shares their secrets with us. So there's a seduction in the word *secret* that can be used for positive purposes. For example, I know that you're probably all familiar with the book and DVD *The Secret*, which has caused a universal conversation about possibility thinking.

I've done many interviews on television and radio about *The Secret*. People ask, "Why is this called a secret, or *the* secret, when it's really not a secret at all?"

That's the whole point: by calling the laws that govern our universe a "secret," human interest becomes stimulated, inquisitiveness spurs people to investigate, especially when a secret is in plain print and one can easily be in on it. But people are shy to ask the question they really want to ask: Is it possible to use a spiritual law to improve the bottom line of my corporation or my business? The answer is not really, because a spiritual principle is not premised upon operational purposes. What this means is that if an organization's bottom line is not service, is not compassion, is not providing a product that serves the greater good, the bottom line may change but there will be no overall improvement. Business will be as usual and any change is merely superficial. We all know that universal law is not a respecter of persons and works alike for all, but the consciousness behind use of the law is what makes a tremendous difference in the bottom line of life.

So *The Secret* sneaks in the back door of spiritual principle by saying that an upside down life can turn right side up. You might say it's a hook that once bitten will lead a person into a deeper understanding of how the laws of the universe operate. It is an entry point that offers an individual the opportunity for further investigation.

Beginning right where you are—and being honest about where that is—whether you are visualizing a better financial life for yourself or yielding to the evolutionary impulse that governs the universe—just say "Yes" to it. Wherever you are in the spiritual continuum of consciousness, just say "Yes" to it, enter it fully, so that you may be ushered into the next step in your unfoldment. And remember, we are always beginners because spiritual awakening is limitless. Fall in love with the secretless Universe and enter the Mystery that joyously awaits your approach.

Contributors

Michael Bernard Beckwith
Michael Bernard Beckwith is the founder of the Agape International Spiritual Center in Los Angeles, California. He is the co-director of the Association for Global New Thought and the Season for Nonviolence. The author of *Inspirations of the Heart*, *Forty Day Mind Fast Soul Feast*, *A Manifesto of Peace*, and *Living from the Overflow*, Beckwith has appeared on *The Oprah Winfrey Show*, *Larry King Live*, and is a featured teacher in the book and DVD *The Secret* as well as the movies *Living Luminaries*, *Pass It On*, and *Millionaire Mind*. You may visit him at *www.agapelive.com*.

Manzel Berlin
Manzel Berlin (Master of Divinity, Emory University) is a Unity Truth student. He is currently writing a book on the paradigm shifts in practical Christianity, particularly how they led to the rejection of slavery in America.

Beverly Saunders Biddle
Rev. Beverly Saunders Biddle, a spiritual life coach, teacher and facilitator, is on the faculty of the Inner Visions Institute for Spiritual Development in Maryland and is a long-time Unity follower.

Rima E. Bonario
Rima Bonario is a freelance writer, teacher and student of Unity and metaphysical teachings, with a passion for helping people discover and live from their divine nature.

Paula Godwin Coppel
Paula Godwin Coppel is vice president of Communications at Unity School of Christianity. She first discovered Unity in 1980 at Unity Church of Portland, Oregon, and is studying to become a licensed Unity teacher.

Wendy Craig-Purcell
Rev. Wendy Craig-Purcell is founding minister and CEO of The Unity Center, a 1500-member spiritual community in San Diego, California.

Ellen Debenport
Rev. Ellen Debenport is senior minister at Unity Church of Dallas and was previously a reporter with United Press International and the *St. Petersburg* (Florida) *Times*. She also serves on the Unity Board of Directors.

Eleanor Fleming

Rev. Eleanor Fleming is an ordained Unity minister and holds a Ph.D. in energy medicine from Holos and Greenwich Universities. She is currently serving as the associate minister at Unity Church Universal in Kansas City, Missouri, and has pioneered New Foundation Unity, a traveling ministry to help people reconnect with Unity's roots.

Lori Fleming

Rev. Lori Fleming is a Unity minister serving Unity Church of Sarasota, Florida.

Shari Franklin

Rev. Shari Franklin, a Unity minister, is the creator and host of "Let There Be Light" on the radio and Internet and the founder of the Transformational Life Center in Mesa, Arizona.

David Friedman

David Friedman, author of the book *The Thought Exchange—New Thought Is More Than What You Think* and the pamphlet *Is Tithing for Me?—A Practical Exploration of Tithing,* divides his time between giving Thought Exchange Workshops and Tithing Talks around the country and his successful career as a songwriter, record producer and concert artist.

Ralph Grzecki

Rev. Ralph Grzecki has been a Unity minister since 1988, after many years as a successful floral business owner in Detroit, and has served ministries in Melbourne, Australia; Warren and Flint, Michigan; Milwaukee, Wisconsin; and now Modesto, California.

Gregory C. Guice

Rev. Gregory C. Guice is a Unity minister and a dedicated teacher and student of the spiritual principles of life as taught in the message of Jesus Christ. He is co-minister at Detroit Unity Temple and serves on the Unity Board of Directors.

Barbara Hadley

Barbara Hadley works at Unity Village and is a prayer chaplain at Unity Church of Overland Park. She volunteers with Complaint Free World and the Humane Society.

Paul Hasselbeck
Rev. Dr. Paul Hasselbeck serves as dean of Spiritual Education at Unity Institute and has a passion for Unity's metaphysical teachings.

Lila Herrmann
Lila Herrmann is a copy editor for Unity School of Christianity and is a new student to New Thought principles.

Art Holt
Rev. Arthur Holt is the minister of Upward Bound Journal, a Unity publishing ministry, and has also served as the minister of Unity Church of Naples, Florida, and editorial director of Unity School of Christianity.

Susan L. Howard
Susan L. Howard is dedicated to Truth in Law and in Spirit. She is a lawyer and student in the Master of Divinity Program, Unity Institute.

Sandra Rae Hymel
Rev. Sandra Rae Hymel, author of two books, *One Thought Can Change Your Life* and *God Is NOT in the Bible*, is a workshop leader and presenter. She serves in the Silent Unity prayer ministry and volunteers with the Association of Unity Churches International.

Kelli Jareaux
Rev. Kelli Jareaux triggers growth through innocence and intimacy. Learn about her and experience her teachings and ministry at *www.GROWContinuum.com*.

Scott Kalechstein
Scott Kalechstein, *www.scottsongs.com*, serves as a New Thought minister, a spiritual counselor, a modern-day troubadour and an inspirational speaker.

Shirley Marshall
Shirley Marshall, Ph.D., human development educator and energy medicine practitioner, guides people in reclaiming their personal and spiritual power. She works in the Telephone Prayer Ministry at Unity Village.

Stephanie Stokes Oliver
Stephanie Stokes Oliver is vice president of Publishing for Unity, and the author of a memoir, *Song for My Father*, and two inspirational nonfiction books: *Seven Soulful Secrets for Finding Your Purpose and Minding Your Mission*, and *Daily Cornbread: 365 Secrets for a Healthy Mind, Body, and Spirit*, which was inspired by Unity's *Daily Word*.

Phillip M. Pierson
Rev. Phillip Pierson is vice president of Unity Institute and spiritual director of Unity School of Christianity.

Kristin Powell
Rev. Kristin Powell serves as minister of Unity Center of Columbia, Missouri, and is the founding minister of Unity Rising, a spiritual adventure travel ministry.

Daniel B. Rebant
Daniel B. Rebant has been active in the Unity movement since 1980 and currently serves as copy supervisor in Unity's Creative Services Department and as associate editor of *Unity Magazine*.

Felicia Searcy
Rev. Felicia Searcy pioneered Unity Church of Life in Murfreesboro, Tennessee, in 2001 and has served as its minister since that time.

Charlotte Shelton
Charlotte Shelton, Ed.D., is president and CEO of Unity School of Christianity. She is the author of *Quantum Leaps: 7 Skills for Workplace ReCreation* and co-author of *The NeXt Revolution: What Gen X Women Want at Work and How Their Boomer Bosses Can Help Them Get It*.

Gary Simmons
Rev. Dr. Gary Simmons, Th.D., is director of Peacemaking Services for the Association of Unity Churches International and author of *The I of the Storm: Embracing Conflict, Creating Peace*, a Unity best seller now in its eighth printing, and *Embrace Tiger, Return to Mountain: Spiritual Conflict Management*.

Walter Starcke
Walter Starcke is an international lecturer, author of seven best-selling books and a member of the Unity Board of Directors.

Sylvia Sumter
Rev. Sylvia Sumter is the senior minister of Unity of Washington, DC; a Board of Directors member of Unity School; and a former chair of Communication Studies and Skills, Unity School for Religious Studies.

Carolyn Thomas
Rev. Carolyn Thomas is an ordained Unity minister, retiree of Unity School of Christianity, author, mandala artist, woodcarver and serves as minister of Creative Path Ministries in Lee's Summit, Missouri.

James Trapp
Rev. James Trapp is the president and CEO of the Association of Unity Churches International. Prior to this position, he was senior minister of Unity on the Bay, Miami, Florida.

Duke Tufty
Rev. Duke Tufty is senior minister of Unity Temple on the Plaza in Kansas City, Missouri, where he has served since 1991. He is also chairman of the Unity Board of Directors.

Bob Uhlar
Rev. Bob Uhlar is a Unity minister and journalist. His Web site is *www.bobuhlar.com*

Ruth Wallace
Rev. Ruth Wallace is a best-selling author who has appeared in print over 50 times. She is a Unity minister and coach who has spoken and taught throughout the United States for over 20 years.

This book has been a labor of love by many people. We at Unity School are deeply grateful to those who contributed to this project, especially to those who provided the meaningful content.

My wish for our readers is that this book will help you not only know more, but also experience more—more joy, peace and prosperity. I hope the wisdom revealed on these pages will unleash an epidemic of insight that enables all of us to take a quantum leap into a new level of abundant living.

—Charlotte Shelton
President and CEO
Unity School of Christianity

Printed in the U.S.A.

B0010-13728-2M-11-07 CG